SPEECH AND LANGUAGE IN THE EARLY YEARS

Speech and Language in the Early Years is an accessible resource, packed full of practical ideas and techniques to support speech and language development in young children.

Learning to communicate is a dynamic process. A child needs a reason to communicate, the motivation to communicate, and, significantly, a responsive communication partner. This book will help you to develop language-rich interactions to facilitate language development in your everyday work and will encourage reflective practice in your setting.

Key features include:

- ❖ Activities and strategies designed for busy educators to dip in and out of as part of everyday practice, promoting speech and language development as well as supporting those with speech, language, and communication needs
- ❖ Templates and techniques for reflective practice, supporting the creation of language-rich environments and encouraging mindful communication
- ❖ Chapters spanning from birth to the transition to school, each exploring different areas of the learning environment

Offering readers the opportunity to extend their skills and confidence in their practice, this book is an essential resource for early years practitioners looking to facilitate quality interactions with the children in their care.

Becky Poulter Jewson has over 25 years of experience working with children and families as a qualified Early Years Lead and is the Director of Early Years and author for Thriving Language Community Interest Company. She has led and developed teams of successful early years educators within children's centres and the private sector. Having owned her own nursery and pre-school, she has developed free flow provision and language-rich learning environments throughout the country. Becky believes that empowering individuals to thrive and helping to create future generations is probably the best career in the world! She is a passionate advocate for early years and supports many further teaching and learning facilities.

Rebecca Skinner qualified as a Speech and Language Therapist in 2001 and is the Director of Speech and Language Therapy and author for Thriving Language Community Interest Company. Alongside her work at Thriving Language, Rebecca works as a Speech and Language Therapist for the NHS, specialising in early years and cleft palate. She is passionate about communication and interaction and the role that the adult plays in the development of this. Rebecca believes that being able to communicate is a basic human right and we must respect all ways of communicating.

SPEECH AND LANGUAGE IN THE EARLY YEARS

CREATING LANGUAGE-RICH LEARNING ENVIRONMENTS

Becky Poulter Jewson and
Rebecca Skinner

Routledge
Taylor & Francis Group
LONDON AND NEW YORK

Cover image: @Getty Images

First published 2022
by Routledge
4 Park Square, Milton Park, Abingdon, Oxon OX14 4RN

and by Routledge
605 Third Avenue, New York, NY 10158

Routledge is an imprint of the Taylor & Francis Group, an informa business
© 2022 Becky Poulter Jewson and Rebecca Skinner

The right of Becky Poulter Jewson and Rebecca Skinner to be identified as authors of this work has been asserted in accordance with sections 77 and 78 of the Copyright, Designs and Patents Act 1988.

All rights reserved. The purchase of this copyright material confers the right on the purchasing institution to photocopy or download pages which bear the support material icon and a copyright line at the bottom of the page. No other parts of this book may be reprinted or reproduced or utilised in any form or by any electronic, mechanical, or other means, now known or hereafter invented, including photocopying and recording, or in any information storage or retrieval system, without permission in writing from the publishers.

Trademark notice: Product or corporate names may be trademarks or registered trademarks, and are used only for identification and explanation without intent to infringe.

British Library Cataloguing-in-Publication Data
A catalogue record for this book is available from the British Library

Library of Congress Cataloging-in-Publication Data
A catalog record has been requested for this book

ISBN: 978-0-367-68970-4 (hbk)
ISBN: 978-0-367-68969-8 (pbk)
ISBN: 978-1-003-13982-9 (ebk)

DOI: 10.4324/9781003139829

Typeset in DIN Pro
by Deanta Global Publishing Services, Chennai, India

Access the Support Material: www.routledge.com/9780367689698

CONTENTS

Acknowledgements		vi
Introduction		1
Chapter 1	Speech and Language Development	3
Chapter 2	Reflective Practice	17
Chapter 3	Birth to 18 Months	31
Chapter 4	18 Months to Two Years	48
Chapter 5	Two to Three Years	74
Chapter 6	Pre-Schoolers	100
Chapter 7	Transitions into School	121
Chapter 8	Speech, Language, and Communication Needs	131
Index		143

ACKNOWLEDGEMENTS

Emily Pearman – thank you for your time and support with our book.

INTRODUCTION

There are multiple theories as to how we develop language but the common theme is that **learning to communicate is an active process** – *it doesn't just happen!*

To become effective communicators, children need a reason to communicate and a desire to do so, and, very importantly, they need an adult to provide responsive feedback. You are in a position to be the best resource for developing a child's communication skills. Mindful interactions and an awareness of the power of everyday situations/experiences will benefit all children who are in your care.

This book aims to work with you to develop language-rich interactions and to stimulate moments of reflection where you and members of the team you work with can consider how you work with children and think about any missed opportunities to facilitate language development.

It has become increasingly difficult to access community speech and language therapy, with referral criteria becoming more specific, and, therefore, early years providers are supporting children's speech and language development more than ever before. This book is going to provide you with techniques and strategies that can be used in your settings to enable you to facilitate speech and language development and also support you as you assist children whose speech and language skills are not developing in the way we would expect.

We will be asking you to reflect. We believe that reflective practice is essential for creating language-rich environments. How do you know something is working and, more importantly, how do you know when something is not working? What would you see that would give you this information? We will provide you with templates and techniques to support your reflective practice.

This book is a resource book for anybody working in early years. It provides useful, easy-to-apply strategies to support speech and language skills from babies to pre-schoolers. The aim of this book is to highlight the fact that adults can be the best resource for supporting children's speech and language development and that they can create language-rich environments without having to spend lots of money.

Due to the age range of children in the early years, each chapter will provide information relevant to specific age ranges: babies, 18 months to two years, two to three years,

Introduction

pre-schoolers. These age ranges have been chosen due to key developmental stages of speech and language.

The chapters will follow a similar format, focusing on the different areas of the learning environment, for example, the outside environment, messy play, role play, and snack time/lunchtime. Each learning area will be explored and the focus will be how to make this a 'language-rich environment' for the children.

We provide top tips and easy-to-implement strategies for promoting speech and language development and also more specific targets and activities that can be used to support children with speech, language, and communication needs.

We want you to really use and enjoy this book in everyday practice. We have created this resource specifically with the early years educator and child at the heart because we understand and respect the dynamic place you hold in creating futures. We celebrate your amazing early years role and hope to develop further understanding, enabling you and future generations of children to be confident in the knowledge that their voice is being listened to and will be heard.

1
SPEECH AND LANGUAGE DEVELOPMENT

What Is Communication?

We communicate in so many ways: spoken words, sign language, gestures, the written word, facial expression, the list goes on!

Communication is a way to share our thoughts and ideas. It is a way to make requests or to express our dislike for something.

It is a way to *connect* with others.

> ### Reflection Point
>
> Take a moment…think about a time when you had some really exciting news to share. Who did you want to tell? What happened? How did they react? How did you feel?
>
> Let's hope this was a positive experience for you. Perhaps the other person shared your excitement, perhaps they showed genuine interest and wanted to know more.
>
> It is in these moments that we can reflect back and value that our message – our communication – was listened to and understood. The result was that we felt 'connected' to that other person and the experience was positive.
>
> What if…
>
> *What if the other person didn't share our excitement?*
>
> *What if the other person didn't listen and started talking about something else?*
>
> *How might that feel?*

> This is a critical point when thinking about communication. A positive experience requires a responsive person who listens and by doing so acknowledges that the person communicating their message is valued.
>
> An excited reaction is obviously not always necessary, a smile may be the appropriate response, but let's be mindful of the communication attempts of the children in our care.
>
> We know that some children will be able to have complex conversations, but we also know that for some children eye pointing is their only means of expressing themselves. As early years professionals we must be aware of and value all types of communication.
>
> Let us strive to create environments where all children are understood.

How Do We Learn Language?

The process of learning language involves acquiring and developing skills which are then built upon and enhanced. We often see the communication pyramid as a way of understanding how language is learned and this suggests that the skills at the bottom must be in place before we can progress to the next layer of learning; but learning to communicate is not a true hierarchical model, as most communication skills will continue to develop and grow as children get older. The communication pyramid is a helpful visual for us to use when we are thinking about what skills we need to focus on with a child who is struggling to communicate. As we can see from the model we wouldn't prioritise focusing on speech sounds if a child is struggling to focus their attention and listening skills. This will be explored further later in the book.

We are going to share with you how children learn language through a 'ten-stage model.' We have deliberately not put specific ages next to each stage, as there is natural variation in the age that children acquire skills, but it is important to know when you should be concerned about speech and language development and you will find information about this in the following chapters.

Stages of Language Development

SOCIAL INTERACTION AND MOTIVATION

Emerging Communicator

- Stage 1 Looking, listening and attention
- Stage 2 Making sounds and taking turns
- Stage 3 Understanding situations
- Stage 4 Pointing and gesturing

Developing Communicator

- Stage 5 Understanding words
- Stage 6 Using single words
- Stage 7 Phrases and sentences

Secure Communicator

- Stage 8 Simple conversations
- Stage 9 Complex conversations
- Stage 10 Speech sounds

Emerging Communicator

This is the first stage of communication development and we can observe the child's communication emerging from birth as the baby cries to 'signal' they are hungry, tired, or need a cuddle.

Stage 1 – Looking, Listening, and Attention

You may have heard the phrase 'pre-requisites for communication development,' but what does this really mean?

Well, we know that talking doesn't just happen and that it is in fact a very complex process.

Pre-requisite skills are the foundations that are needed to support later language learning, and children develop these skills from birth.

Hearing is an important part of this process. Language is typically learned through exposure to sounds, and it is vital to identify any hearing difficulties as soon as possible to ensure that support can be put in place. In the United Kingdom, the Newborn Hearing Screening Programme helps to identify babies with moderate, severe, or profound hearing loss as soon as possible. Children may pass this test but go on to experience glue ear at a later stage.

For ears to work properly, the middle ear needs to be kept full of air. The air travels through the eustachian tube, which runs from the back of the throat to the middle ear. If the eustachian tube becomes blocked, air can't enter the middle ear. When this happens, the cells lining the middle ear begin to produce fluid.

With fluid blocking the middle ear, it becomes harder for sound to pass through to the inner ear – making quieter sounds difficult to hear. It can be like listening to the world with your fingers stuck in your ears. This is glue ear.

The following are common signs of glue ear: changes in behaviour, becoming tired and frustrated, a lack of concentration, preferring to play alone, and not responding when called. These signs can often be mistaken for rudeness or being 'naughty.' As a result, children with glue ear may be misunderstood or labelled as 'difficult.'

Glue ear will often resolve on its own, but prolonged episodes of glue ear can result in speech and language difficulties. If you have any concerns about hearing, speak to the child's parents and request a referral for a hearing test.

Listening is a skill to be developed. We all know of people with good hearing who struggle to listen. Babies are learning how to listen from birth; they learn to listen to voices and they learn which voices are important to them.

Listening and attention are skills which are often referred to together and 'looking' is another skill which fits well in this group.

In this first stage, a baby is learning to look and focus their attention. From birth, a baby will watch their parent's face and again will learn to discriminate between faces and work out which faces are important to them. This skill of looking will enable the baby to develop eye contact and provide them with the opportunity to gain information from the parent's/adult's face.

A child who has difficulty looking at and attending to their parent's face when they are talking will have fewer opportunities to hear language and words and it will be more difficult for the child to attach meaning to those words.

Listening and attention skills emerge at this stage, but they will continue to develop throughout the other stages.

Stage 2 – Making Sounds and Taking Turns

Children start to make sounds and noises before they learn to say words.

At this stage a child is experimenting with sounds, moving their lips and tongue (articulators). As they continue to experiment and play with sounds, they will eventually attach meaning to these sounds.

Early turn-taking skills emerge at this stage, with parents/carers noticing the child's smiles, vocalisations, and movements and then imitating the action or adding a word to the interaction. By waiting/pausing after the adult's response, the child is given the opportunity to repeat their smile, vocalisation, and movement, creating a shared interaction and an early turn-taking experience.

This is an important stage for communication development as the child is learning that when they do something (make a noise, move, smile), an adult responds. The child is learning early 'cause and effect' and most importantly, in that moment the child knows that they matter.

> ### Reflection Point
>
> Just think for a moment...what could happen if the child's vocalisations, movements, and smiles went unnoticed?
>
> What might happen if the child doesn't get positive feedback at this stage?

> The role of the adult in this stage is so crucial. A child at this stage needs the adults around them to be observant and responsive as they develop these early yet fundamental skills for communication development.

Making Sounds

During this stage, babies will begin to vocalise and then babble.

Vocalisation refers to those early sounds that babies make: gurgling and vowel-type sounds. Babbling is the reduplicated strings of consonants and vowels which begin to sound like real words, such as 'mu mu mu"' and 'da da da"da da.'

What is important here is that initially the baby is still playing with their sounds and experimenting with their articulators but the 'tuned in' adult has the opportunity to attach meaning. For example, when the baby says, 'mu mu mu,' and 'mummy' appears; happy, smiling, and engaged, modelling the word 'mummy,' baby begins to realise that their sounds have meaning and power. This doesn't happen in that one moment but over time with repetition and consistent responses and reactions from the adults.

Stage 3 – Understanding Situations

In the first 12 months, understanding is based on cues in the environment, such as direction of the adult's eye gaze, pointing, gesture, facial expression, and body language.

At this stage the child is learning that the sound of running water means it is 'bath time,' or that the sound of voices getting louder means that another person is approaching.

Children learn their first routines and this predictability and familiarity are important for learning keywords and creating a safe and secure environment for the child. Repetition of keywords in routine situations provides a solid foundation for further vocabulary development.

Stage 4 – Pointing and Gesturing

This is a crucial part of the 'learning language' journey.

Babies and young children point for a number of reasons: to make requests, to share an experience with someone else, or to draw attention to someone or something. The key point here is that the child is now demonstrating communicative intent. The child's ability to point to something to draw an adult's attention to it has real significance. The child is beginning to develop joint attention, an important feature of social interaction.

Difficulties with joint attention result in a child having fewer opportunities to learn about objects in their environment. It is by looking at things together and an adult commenting or talking about what is being looked at that helps the child to learn new words and attach meaning to those words, for example adult and child are looking out of the window at a bus driving by and the adult models 'bus.'

Pointing is just one type of non-verbal communication; at this stage we may also see waving or lifting arms up to an adult in a request to be picked up.

Developing Communicator

Throughout this stage, the child develops from non-verbal to verbal communicator and will generally have more success at communicating their message to familiar and also unfamiliar people. We have described these next stages as 'developing,' as the child is still very dependent on the 'tuned in' adults around them to model, extend, and teach in order to progress to the 'secure' stage of language development.

Stage 5 – Understanding Words

We touched on this in stage 4 – children typically learn to attach meaning to a word through interaction with others. Through joint attention (attending to the same thing at the same time as another person), a child is provided with the name of the item under focus and through repetition and consistency (use of the same word as opposed to variations, for example 'horse,' 'horsie,' 'gee gee') the child learns the specific vocabulary and begins to attach meaning to the word.

It is at this stage that we can observe that children typically understand more than they can say.

We observe this understanding in the child's behaviour – they may look towards the object/person that the adult names. They may be able to select an object on request – 'where's your ball?'

Stage 6 – Using Single Words

We typically hear first words around 12 to 18 months. We all know children who have said their first words earlier than this and there is such variation.

Children need to hear words over and over again before they can begin to understand and use them. It is usual that first words will be toys, food, animals, and people that the child is interested in. Children need to be motivated to use their words, which is why you will observe that their first words will be words that are important and meaningful for that individual child.

During this stage children will learn that they can use their words to request ('biscuit'), to refuse/reject ('no'), to show you something they are interested in ('car'). The adult has a crucial role to play at this stage – children need us to *respond and repeat*! By doing this, we show the child that we have heard them, we value what they are saying, they matter to us, and so, importantly, we show them that when you communicate your message, something happens.

Stage 7 – Phrases and Sentences

Children typically need to be using 50 words before they will progress to this next stage of combining words and forming simple sentences. Children will use keywords to convey their message, for example 'me juice,' 'daddy gone.'

At this stage children will learn different 'types' of words. Verbs (action words: dance, jump) are especially important for building sentences. Children need to hear language models to support the development in this stage. They have a 'bank' of single words and through listening to those around them (commenting, reading, singing) they will begin to experiment putting words together and again that pattern of *respond and repeat* from the adult shows the child that their message is valued and they have been understood.

Secure Communicator

Secure communicators have made the communication connection – they understand that their words have meaning and power and can express their needs, wants, and preferences with a range of people in a variety of contexts. There is still more learning to be done, but we know that developing language skills actually continues into adulthood, as we are all still learning the meaning of new words we encounter.

Stage 8 – Simple Conversations

Having a conversation is a process of turn-taking. When a conversation works well, one speaker has a turn, then the other speaker has a turn, and usually the speakers stay on a particular topic. Learning to have a conversation is an important skill for children to develop as this skill enables children to develop friendships, to ask for what they want, and to be listened to. A 'good' conversation requires the speaker to express themselves clearly and also be able to listen well.

At this stage, children can now express themselves in sentences. Vocabulary has grown and a knowledge of grammar is developing.

There are many skills that are needed to have conversations: children need to learn how to start a conversation, take turns, listen, and know when to stop talking. We all need to learn the skills of understanding what another person already knows and how much we need to tell them; this is a complex skill that continues to develop and to be refined throughout childhood (and sometimes adulthood).

Simple conversations will often emerge when a child wants to share something with you that interests them. They may invite you to join their play and this gives you the opportunity to listen to what they say, follow their lead, and engage in a simple conversation. They may start an interaction with a request 'more biscuit mummy'; again, you can use this opportunity to engage in a simple conversation – you could present a choice of two biscuits or use the moment to describe the biscuit and what you both enjoy about biscuits.

At this stage, the child may move quickly from one topic to another, but simple conversation will often be about the child's everyday world around them (people, food, toys).

As has been said before, the adult's role is to *respond* so that the child learns that their communication is valued and that these simple conversations are rewarding and enjoyable.

Stage 9 – Complex Conversations

Complex conversation is being able to talk about past events. It is also being able to reason, predict, and express empathy. At this stage children will begin to understand more abstract topics such as emotions and culture. To engage in complex conversations, children need to develop the skills required to keep an interaction going.

This is quite a leap in terms of development and will take time; we may see complex conversation emerging from the age of three, but typically these skills are more evident as the child approaches the age of four years. Remember that children watch and will learn how to have these conversations by watching how we as adults have conversations. They will be observing our vocabulary, body language, facial expressions, and tone of voice – it is important to remember this!

Stage 10 – Speech Sounds

Speech sounds – these are the sounds we produce when we say words.

We have already seen how complex a process it is learning to talk and learning how to move various parts of our mouth in order to articulate specific sounds can be a challenge and takes time to master.

Speech and Language Development

Whilst we have placed this at stage 10, we know that speech sounds start developing from stage 2 when the child starts making sounds and this continues to develop throughout all the stages. We have put speech sounds as the last stage because it is typically the last thing that speech and language therapists will work on if the child is still struggling at other stages of communication development.

The majority of speech sounds are produced by creating a stream of air which moves from the lungs through the nose or mouth (depending on which sound we are going to say).

Try and talk whilst holding your breath – what happens?

Some sounds require vocal cord vibration (vocal cords are located in the larynx/voice box), some don't, and other sounds are produced by changing the shape of our mouths; it really is a complex process and something we tend to do without much thought or attention.

At this point, let's remind ourselves of some terminology:

- ❖ Consonant – a speech sound which is produced when the flow of air from the lungs is momentarily stopped (our lips coming together when we say 'p') or when there is a very narrow gap which makes the air hiss as it passes (our top teeth and lower lip when saying 'f').
    Examples of consonants; m, n, p, b, t, d, f, s, k, g, sh, ch.
- ❖ Oral consonant – a speech sound produced as air moves through the mouth (p, b, t, d, f, s, k, g, sh, ch).
- ❖ Nasal consonant – a speech sound produced as air moves through the nose (m, n, ng).
- ❖ Vowel – a speech sound produced by changing the shape of our mouth ('ee,' 'oo,' 'ah').
- ❖ Articulators – parts of the vocal tract which have a role in the production of a speech sound: lips, teeth, tongue.

Reflection Point

Take a moment...say the following sounds:

m

b

f

t

k

oo

What is happening in your mouth?

How are you saying each sound?

Think about where the air is travelling – mouth or nose?

Which articulators are moving? Is there any contact in your mouth? Which parts of your mouth are moving in order to produce the sound?

Ages and Stages

This chart shows the approximate age we would expect to hear specific speech sounds.

Remember it is a guide. For more information on when to be concerned about speech sound development, please refer to Chapters 3–6 depending on the age of the child you are concerned about.

Age	Sounds you may hear
1:6 – 2:0	m, p, b
2:0 – 2:6	m, p, b, t, d, w
2:6 – 3:0	m, p, b, t, d, w, f, s, y, k, g, h, l
3:0 – 3:6	m, p, b, t, d, w, f, s, y, k, g, h, l, sh, ch
3:6 – 4:6	m, p, b, t, d, w, f, s, y, k, g, h, l, sh, ch, j, z, r
4:6 Onwards	m, p, b, t, d, w, f, s, y, k, g, h, l, sh, ch, j, z, r, th

We would expect all speech sounds to be developed and in use by eight years of age.

Reference: www.thrivinglanguage.co.uk/speechsounds

As children grow, the way they say a word will naturally change and it is important to remember that making errors is to be expected as a part of typical development.

We have talked about how speech sounds are produced and that seemed complicated enough, but we also need to know which sound we must say for a word to be produced accurately.

Take a moment...

You are going to answer the question 'would you like tea or coffee?'

Imagine you have a filing cabinet in your brain, you need to select the file for 'coffee,' and then you need to find the section of that file which details that it starts with a 'c,' that's followed by an 'o' and an 'f,' and that ends with an 'ee.' You then need to work out which bits of your mouth you need to move to produce the sound.

Wow – this is complex and sometimes we wonder how anyone learns to speak clearly at all, but they do!

Even before birth, babies are exposed to the human voice. We talk to our babies and our children and they grow and develop their own communication skills. So why do some children struggle to speak clearly?

For some children a medical diagnosis such as a cleft palate, cerebral palsy, or hearing impairment may have a direct association with their speech sound difficulties, however for many children, a speech sound difficulty exists without an obvious cause.

It is possible that some speech sound difficulties will resolve without intervention; others may persist and require specialist support.

It is important to identify speech sound difficulties as persistent difficulties may impact self-confidence, social interaction, and the development of literacy skills. If you have any questions/concerns, seek advice from a speech and language therapist.

Throughout All Stages – Social Interaction and Motivation

A key point to remember is that children learn and thrive when they feel safe, secure, and listened to, which tells us that the emotional environment is just as important as the physical environment.

So, why is social interaction important for language learning and why is it a skill that develops from stage 1 and continues to develop throughout the stages detailed here and beyond?

Social interaction is the process by which we act and react to others. During the ten stages of early communication development, social interaction is important for developing an understanding of social cues – recognising facial expressions and other non-verbal communication. It is an important skill in the development of building connections and relationships with others.

The common theme through each of the ten stages is that the development occurs through a dynamic process. We have referred to the role of the adult but social interaction with peers is also extremely important.

If children learned language through 'input' and imitation alone, then we could turn on the television and allow children to 'absorb' language this way, but we know this isn't enough. Children need people around them to listen, interpret, and *respond and repeat* in order to develop their language skills.

Building relationships is key and a 'tuned in' adult can observe what motivates a child, what they are really interested in, and how they play. The adult can then add language to the interaction that is both meaningful and interesting to the child.

Meaningful social interaction with a child is a basis for language development.

What Is a Speech and Language Therapist and What Is Their Role in Early Years?

Speech and language therapists work with adults and children – assessing and treating speech, language, and communication difficulties as well as difficulties with eating, drinking, and swallowing.

In early years, speech and language therapists work closely with families, early years professionals, and other health professionals such as health visitors.

Children learn through play and speech and language therapists will often use the information that parents/carers and early years professionals have about a child, their interests, and their motivations in order to create an individualised plan.

It is important to note that with young children, speech therapy is not something that is 'done to' the child. Therapy will often involve working closely with parents/carers to develop strategies that the adults can implement in order to support language development.

What Is the Role of the Early Years Professional in Supporting Children with Speech, Language, and Communication Needs?

Early years professionals have a vital role in children's future outcomes. Through working with the child and following their ideas and interests, we can then see how to help the child to develop and progress.

To robustly support children with speech, language, and communication needs, we base our practice on what we know about the child and what interests them, and this then becomes a focused and natural way forward to embed mutual understanding.

We all know that we learn much better when something interests us – this is the same for children. Start with what you know, then observe and create interesting and exciting provocation that motivates the child and that the child can take ownership of.

Our specialism in early years should be to understand the individual child, problem-solve together, and be an advocate for the child's voice to be heard however they decide to communicate. Create a joint plan that is realistic and will work, liaise with other people and professionals who know the child well and enable the child to succeed.

Just a note of caution here, as an early years professional you are not expected to take a child out for one-one specialist speech and language therapy; as previously mentioned, this is not a 'done to' objective. Plans should be enabled through natural play and real life to enable positive steps for the child. Always remember quality interactions and really listening to the child is a skilled and vital role for the early years professional. Children need autonomy and trust and to be given the power to succeed.

> **Reference**
>
> Thriving Language, Ages and Stages Speech Sounds, www.thrivinglanguage.co.uk/speechsounds

2
REFLECTIVE PRACTICE

What Is 'Reflective Practice'?

Many of us have heard this term used in our working lives but do we really understand what it means and why it is relevant to our everyday working lives?

To reflect is to think about an action or event that has happened and crucially to consider how things could have been done differently. It is equally as important to think about what worked well and what should therefore be repeated.

It is important to note that this process is different from merely looking back at an event and recalling what happened. Reflective practice, as mentioned above, is about looking back at an event or action and learning lessons from what did or did not work. This is not always an easy, or indeed comfortable thing to do, especially if we are evaluating our own actions and know that we didn't get things quite right.

Let's take a moment right now to stop and remember 'perfect does not exist,' we are all human and there will be times when something doesn't work well or didn't lead to the outcome we were hoping for. By reflecting on our practice, we can explore the reasons for this and, importantly, use this knowledge to develop our practice, which will lead to better experiences for the children we are working with.

Whose Responsibility Is It?

There is a statutory expectation that all early years practitioners will be given regular supervision sessions. These sessions are a good opportunity to discuss your strengths and to consider areas that you have identified as areas for further development.

Our managers have a responsibility to support us with our professional development, however we have a duty of care to the children we are educating. We must accept that ultimately it is our own individual responsibility to reflect and evaluate our practice and, crucially, be aware of not doing things one way just because they have always been done that way.

If you work in a more solitary environment, such as childminding, seek out peer support through local childminding networks so that you can have these professional conversations.

How Do You Do It?

We must acknowledge here that reflective practice is not just about thinking. It is important to develop an understanding of the theory that underpins our practice and to explore what motivates our colleagues and explore ideas together.

Here are our five top tips for developing your skills in reflective practice:

- **Read and research** – learn more about the theories and research which underpin our practice.
- **Communicate** – share your views and experiences with others and ask questions…why do your colleagues do what they do?
- **Observe** – what's happening around you? Take time to stop and really look.
- **Emotions** – consider how you are feeling. Are there any triggers which result in you experiencing positive or negative emotions? We need to understand how we manage our feelings and emotions.
- **Time** – this process takes time, however it is important that we give ourselves permission to value the time spent thinking about work.

Reflective practice can be an individual or a group activity, but it can sometimes be tricky to know where to start.

We know how important adult-child interaction is for successful communication development and we will explore this in greater detail throughout this book. With this in mind, let's start the process of reflective practice by thinking about how we interact with children and what our strengths are.

This template is a good place to start. Take some time and look through the statements. Consider how they relate to you as a practitioner.

Remember – this is not a test!

Be honest as you rate yourself against the statements. You do not have to share this information with anyone else but it can be useful to discuss your strengths and areas to develop with your colleagues so that you can support each other with your professional development.

Reflective Practice

Practitioner Rating Scale

Think about the following statements and rate yourself.

How often do you...

	Never	Sometimes	Often	Always
Position yourself to be at the same level as the child				
Use natural gestures to reinforce language				

	Never	Sometimes	Often	Always
Talk slowly enough for the child to understand				
Give the child time to talk/ ensure the child has time to respond				
Respond to the child so they know they have been understood (look, gesture, word, repeat what they have said)				

	Never	Sometimes	Often	Always
Let the child choose the toy/activity				
Follow what the child wants to do with the toy				
Wait for the child to start interacting (child may look at the adult, gesture, make a sound/noise)				

	Never	Sometimes	Often	Always
Comment on what the child is doing – label objects/ actions/feelings				
Ask lots of questions				
Use the child's name to get their attention				
Expand on the child's utterance – repeat/add word(s)				

Why Do We Need to Do This?

This all seems very time-consuming and just another thing to have to do, so why does it matter?

Well...we have already touched on this: it matters because the children matter!

We must always look at what we are doing and how we are doing it. All children are unique, and they deserve educators who are constantly reflecting and updating their skills and knowledge.

The Practitioner Rating Scale is a good place to start – once you have completed the rating scale, take some time to look through your results. Think about where your strengths are and take a moment to celebrate those.

Your next step is to identify where you would like to develop.

As mentioned, the Practitioner Rating Scale is there to support you to reflect on your adult-child interaction skills. Which elements can you identify as being an area you could develop?

Let's be careful not to try and change everything in one go. You are creating your own 'next step' and it needs to be a realistic and achievable target, like those you would set for your 'key children.'

As you progress through this book, we will explore each of the strategies on the Practitioner Rating Scale in more detail, so you have a full understanding of why they matter for communication development.

As with any 'target' or 'next step' we need to know how to achieve this and how we will know when we have achieved this. This is where peer observation can be an extremely useful tool, and this is what we are going to explore next.

What Is Peer Observation?

For deeper understanding of this we are going to start with what it should not be!

When we hear this term, it is sometimes a cause for concern amongst early years teams, especially when related to Ofsted 'a joint peer observation with the inspector.' The other reason for a negative experience is when a peer observation is used to 'tell people off' and not used constructively or shared with the individual being observed. Peer observations should not be a 'done to' activity; they should always be constructed with reflection and thought. What do we want to know from a peer observation?

> **Reflection Point**
>
> Why do we need to be observed?
>
> In early years we observe children all the time; we therefore know what an observation is.
>
> However, do we really know what it feels like to be observed?
>
> **Take a little time to think about this next statement:**
>
> *Do you ask for the child's permission to observe them? Do you share with them what you have written about them?*
>
> To understand reflective, meaningful peer observations, we need to look at our whole practice of how we observe others.

A peer observation enables reflective practice by understanding what you and your colleagues (peers) are doing well, what you could improve on, and how connected you are in your work with the children.

What environments do you excel in and what is your level of engagement in your career?

One of the most crucial elements of a peer observation in early years is to look at your quality interactions, your teaching, and how you extend children's play and ideas without changing their thoughts. How to gain confidence in provocations and comments rather than questions is a key element of peer observations; if you really know how you practice then you can continually improve.

All genuinely great teachers are non-static, they are always learning. This is a fantastic life skill and a lesson for children and your peers. A practitioner who embeds a love of reflection, improvement and lifelong learning into their practice will create an environment in which children will thrive.

Think about these points when developing your peer observation template:

Reflective Practice

Quality interaction teaching provocation	Thriving practice	Reflections and discussion	Overall points scale 1–10 (always discuss, be honest, and find a way to improve)
Starting point: Understanding what quality interactions look like: • In practice • In leadership • In your team • With children • With other professionals • With families What do quality interactions feel like? Would you like to be a child in your early years environment? What do you believe teaching children involves? Do you make time for children's ideas? Is your routine flexible? Whose agenda do you follow? Do you think every moment is a natural teaching moment? Do you know each child well? Do you know what will help each child to progress? Are you confident to use provocation in your practice and follow child-led ideas?	How engaged and invested in your practice are you? Do you believe children have their own ideas that are valuable in their learning? Do you enjoy working with children? Do you recognise the importance of the role you have in children's futures? Do you listen? Do you comment?	What happened? Would you change what you did? How could you improve your practice? (remember everyone is always learning and improving) Do you feel professional? Do you feel that you were teaching? What did the child gain from your practice? Was there choice for the child? Were the child's ideas valued?	1. No interaction. 2. Not aware of surroundings or child's ideas. 3. Elements of teaching are not present yet. 4. Care for the child is starting to be shown. 5. Some interactions mostly adult-led. 6. Adult listened and interacted, however the child was not engaged. 7. Adult gave autonomy and listened well to the child. 8. Adult gave autonomy, connected when invited, and listened well. 9. Adult used gestures, body language, listened and commented well. Gave autonomy and space where needed. Adult trusted the child's ideas and voice. 10. Adult used positive and genuine gestures and body language, listened and commented well. Gave autonomy, space, and time. Extended through child-led ideas and provocation. Adult trusted the child, *listened to their voice, and heard their ideas. Child engaged deeply in play. Adult respected the child and their colleagues. *listened to the child's voice however they chose to communicate.

How Do We Do Peer Observations?

A peer observation will need permission from the person you are observing. You can ask the team if they would like you to observe them throughout the day and then give feedback. This may lead to more natural observations. Be respectful of people's self-esteem when observing as some people tend to freeze a little, others may behave in a more exaggerated way than usual and typical practice may be affected. We use peer observations to improve confidence in practice and build self-esteem. Remember that lifelong learning and understanding of how we can positively improve will enhance not only our lives but also the children we work with.

Here is a bit of a myth buster: it does not have to be the team leader who observes. It is much better to enable all the team 'peers' to be the observer at various times. This way role modelling and thriving practice can be embedded and understood by everyone. If we know what we are looking for this demystifies the concern of being observed. You are actively sharing the power and understanding, the result of this will be much richer evidence of shared reflective practice.

You will want to feel confident when carrying out a joint observation, so practising this in a natural way is key to understanding it. The more you and your team are observed and observe each other, the better you will all understand what quality interactions and reflective practice look like. You are not expecting to be perfect at every aspect of practice and as we work with children, we can never understand every aspect of what might happen next or where practice might take us.

An example of this could be if a child hurts another child when an observation is taking place. What would you do? We bet you are saying 'what I would always do'; well, yes you are right. Natural, brilliant practice of engaging with the child and ensuring the hurt child is well, asking for another practitioner to help if needed, seeing what would help the child who is hurt, engaging with the child who hurt him, and seeing if she can help think what might make him better. Quite often when we do this in practice, the child who has hurt another child will go and get the other child a toy or may want to hug them.

Right at the start we mentioned 'every moment is a teaching moment' – one of our key thriving points. Here the teaching element is to develop and teach empathy by being empathetic and helping the children to understand their feelings. Peer observations do not have to be perfect – they need to be real-life natural practice and serve as a key reflective tool to enable awesome practitioners to change lives for the better.

Practise joint observations with all your colleagues and discuss your findings together. Making time for peer observations can be a sticking block, however using this time well and coming out of an office and into practice is extremely beneficial. If you are all counted in numbers all the time, then giving children time, space, and autonomy to play will enable peer observations.

We could say 'practice makes perfect', however in this case we are not looking for perfect, we are looking for 'practice creates understanding' and 'practice grows confidence.' We recommend you give it a go and enhance yours and your peers' professional reflective journeys.

Understanding Your Environment

Understanding your environment – by this we mean really starting to explore the purpose of the environment you create for and with children.

One of the main points here is that as professionals we create spaces for children that we believe they would like. We follow government frameworks that show us what should be taught in the environment and often these areas become a physical presence where children play.

Let us look at this in a different way, from the children's viewpoint. We first need to observe and see what the children are really interested in. We need to watch and listen to be a successful communicator and educator. The children are constantly giving clues and ideas of who they are throughout their play; we just need to observe, reflect, and communicate that we have understood them.

How Can You Look at Your Environment Critically?

> **Reflection Point**
>
> When you are in your environment:
>
> What do you see?
>
> What does it feel like?
>
> Is it somewhere you want to be?
>
> Does it feel calm?
>
> Do you feel loved and listened to?
>
> Do you feel like you matter?

The answers to these questions are the starting point for how you create and look at your environment critically.

Let us add another level of understanding reflective practice in the environment...

- ❖ If there were no toys at all in your environment, what would you and the children do? How would you teach and engage the children?
- ❖ If you and the children were in a field with lots of space and natural surroundings, would you need any toys?

By examining what atmosphere and energy you bring to your environment you start to create critical thinking. If you work with a team or work independently, it is so important to take the time to reflect on these ideas. Now as we have mentioned, it is not always easy to create an environment of change, some people may embrace it wholeheartedly and some may not. Communication and having an understanding that everyone has their own ideas is a great starting point. We must always come back to the real reason behind our reflections, to enable better futures for the children we work with. This should underpin every decision we make!

Creating an inclusive, kind, and wonderful space to be educated in is something you do with the children. It is created through their eyes. You use your skills to add provocation, comments, and quality interactions. Early years is a creative industry, so be mindful that we do not create our own ideas and forget about the children's. By all means paint your own picture alongside a child, using comments and authentic body language to show you are really engaged, this could enable the child to see that you value the time to just be alongside them. A little reminder here, children also need their own autonomy at times to engage deeply in their play ideas, discover who they are, and have freedom of expression.

Why Do We Need to Do This?

If we think of every opportunity throughout our day with the children as a teaching opportunity, rather than a routine of things that must be done, this starts to change the way we view education.

We are reflecting on ourselves as part of the environmental influence, for example, 'putting coats on' – now this can be a brilliant time for really getting to know the child and to help teach them an independent skill. Or, it can be a bit of a muddle and a rush, where everyone tries to get their coat on and the busy practitioner ends up doing up coats quickly to get to the next part of the routine in the day.

Even from this little element of reflection in practice, we can see that calmness, patience, and self-help skills are a much better lesson to learn and understand. The child needs to see this and feel co-regulated. For early years, this can mean how we practice with and around children.

This is worth exploring further as self-regulation for the child cannot happen without co-regulation from a trusted adult.

> **Reflection Point**
>
> Environmental co-regulation:
>
> ❖ Does the child willingly come to you for help when needed?
> ❖ What does the child's body language tell you?
> ❖ What are the sound levels like in your environment?
> ❖ Does anyone raise their voice or shout?
> ❖ Do you and your colleagues make time to ask each other how you are feeling?
> ❖ Do you feel supported?
> ❖ Are gestures and body language from all the adults in your environment positive and respectful?
> ❖ If a child makes a mistake, do they feel supported to learn from this?
> ❖ If a child hits another child or adult, are they supported at that moment in time or are they shamed?
>
> NB: Asking a child who is dysregulated to calm down or think about what they have done or sit in time out is not co-regulation and will not help self-regulation. Helping them to regulate their emotions through your calmness and empathy will work.
>
> When the child is calm and emotionally regulated that is the time to talk to them about their and the other child's feelings. If this is continual and the child is often dysregulated you will need to reflect on this further, speak to line managers and families, and sign post to other professionals where needed.
>
> Adults and children who are dysregulated will change the feeling of the environment and this will need to be discussed openly and honestly.

We all know what it feels like to walk into an environmental atmosphere of negativity. This is not how any early years or educational environment should feel and this always needs addressing.

Key Reflection Point

Remember – we are creating futures and shaping brains through the environments we create.

How Do You Identify 'Sizzling Spots' and 'Redundant Areas'?

Let us move on now to the physical environment. Our reflection here is around what is used and what is not.

Have a look at the example template. Discover and tap into unused environmental spaces.

You can use this idea to really personalise the understanding of your inside and outside spaces.

Area	Reflections What did we observe?	Sizzling spot?	Reflection What can we do? Why?	Who is going to do this? What will we need?
The sandpit	Lots of children wanting to use this space at the same time, a few disagreements happening	**Totally** Quite often Not really Not at all	Team reflection (chat) about making this area bigger or two areas. To enable deeper levels of engagement in play and fewer disagreements.	The children will be asked if they want to help and explain why this is needed. The team from pre-school – we will start tomorrow. Logs, branches, or a wooden pallet, plastic to put on the ground (bin bags would work), sand.

Reflective Practice

| The book area | Two children accessed this throughout the morning, they didn't stay long in this area | Totally
Quite often
Not really
Not at all | Team reflection (chat):
Is this just a certain time of the day, is this used better at other times?
Is the book area welcoming, cosy, and relaxed? What are the resources?
Is this area being role modelled by an adult?
It is important to develop this area to create a love of books and quality interactions between adults and children. | Create an environment of relaxation.
Add fairy lights and blankets.
Swap books around and look at child-led interests.
Ask the children what they would like and why they don't go in the book corner?
Adult to be present and mindful – offer to read with the child. Remember the process – this is not to get to the end of the book. This is to interact and connect and follow children's lead, comments, ideas, and provocation. |

Once you have observed these areas reflect on what information you have. If you work with a team, ask another colleague to observe again at a different time. This will enable you to have richer evidence and understanding for change. If you work on your own, unpick what you have seen and think about what your next step is.

NB: Remember to include the children, tell them what you are writing and what you are trying to discover. They might like to have a sheet on a clipboard to help you.

Ask them why they do not play in this area. Ask them why they go to the popular areas. Keep giving the children the ownership of their environment so they will feel trusted and empowered.

Gaining confidence and decision-making skills, trying out teamwork and understanding new words is a fantastic opportunity for the children. We can never say enough that '**every moment is a teaching moment**' – we are all learning every day. It is important that the children know that you make mistakes and that you do not know everything. However, with reflection together you will know where to find the answers. You are now in the process of empowering a generation of 'Thinkers' with confidence to ask questions and problem solve when they don't know.

We would introduce the term 'Reflection' to the children from a young age and model what it means in everyday environmental language.

Here are a few reflective examples you might like to say and respond with:

- I am reflecting on... (what you said, what you did, your idea, the playroom, tidy up time, etc.)
- I am thinking about...
- I thought about that and...

Commenting to the child:

- You look like you are thinking
- You seem to be reflecting on that idea
- You really thought about that
- You look worried
- You seem sad
- You look pleased
- You tried so hard
- I know it's frustrating when...

The more in tune you are with reflection and thinking about your choices, ideas, the way you practice and speak to the children, the more in tune and reflective they will become.

What do you and your team, if you have one, want your environment to be, to do, and to achieve? There must always be thought behind everything you do. Now, we know this might seem a bit arduous but you are in charge of children's futures, you have the power, you are a professional (you do not need to have qualifications to view yourself as a professional), so why would you not stop to think about your teaching environment?

Time – yes, we agree! Early years are remarkably busy, but without reflecting on your environment how can you teach properly?

Your environment is part of the triangle of teaching and it is crucial you enable it.

Parent

Child

Environment   Practitioner

Reflective Practice

The worry about the time to do this can stem from rigid routines – 'we must do this, at this time,' 'nappy time now,' 'let's all put our coats on and go out.' Flexible routines are the ally of early years professionals; they create 'in the moment' teaching and understanding of the unique child. Sitting, listening, reflecting, being interested in the child, and giving them your time are the best elements of teaching you will ever do.

We have all seen tired-looking classrooms, that are too bright, dull, or just cluttered. Faded things stuck to the wall that have been there for ages. When you reflect and create your environment you are building the atmosphere, vibe, care, and professional love. Our recommendation is to start somewhere today, just one little reflection, one little positive change, and talk to the children about their ideas for change.

3
BIRTH TO 18 MONTHS

Babies – aren't they fascinating! They learn so much. They learn to roll over, sit, crawl, walk, and communicate, amongst other things!

During this stage, babies will go from vocalising to babbling to saying their first words. We need to know how to promote and enjoy each of these stages and how to support these babies to move on to the next stage of communication development.

There is so much learning that takes place during this stage. Babies' brains are growing and changing rapidly, and their development is so dependent on the interactions and play opportunities that they experience. We, as the adults in their lives, have a key role to play here and we must always remember that babies are not passive; rather, they are active learners and need us to help them thrive.

Play and the Environment

The physical environment – Let's take a moment to reflect...

What does the environment look like?

Is it working, how do we know it is working?

What would it look like if the environment wasn't working?

The baby's physical environment is key to learning and understanding new language. Overstimulation, where it is too loud and busy, can become a distraction. Babies require calmness of tone and a physical atmosphere in which they feel safe.

Once a baby feels safe and that they matter they can begin to learn. Trust is built up by really understanding the baby and what they are communicating to you. Look out for gestures, expressions, eye pointing, and a generally engaged and calm interaction. Quality interactions are not done *to* the baby; they are a joint process of return and serve. So, you are working from the starting point of what enables the baby to feel safe and professionally loved.

Birth to 18 Months

For babies to thrive, they require consistency but also flexibility. Routine is important, but we must remember that all babies are individual and will need to be understood as such, with routines being adjusted to suit their needs.

Having a flexible routine allows for really listening and understanding the baby at more than a functional level. Nappy times are carried out when the baby needs it, as are sleep times. The more you understand the baby, the more the baby will relax and learn.

Activities stem from what stage the baby is at and what they feel comfortable with, so introduce new environments slowly. A baby can explore the outside or you can bring the outside inside by adding 'child-friendly' plants which could be hung by the window and enjoy the movement as they catch the breeze.

To bring the outside in, here are just a few ideas: if it is safe to do so, have mud, water, wet clay, and sand to explore; a wooden bowl of spinach leaves and some cooled tea bags, exploring fruit tea water (check for allergies). This all encourages new discussion and comments.

Remember, you do not need to over plan. Work with introducing new ideas at the baby's pace; often they will want to repeat, repeat, repeat – this is when the baby's brain is creating connections. For instance, think about water play 'splashing, patting, sploshing' with hands. To start with you model this slowly and wait and then repeat. There are no points and educational gains for getting all of the babies to join in if they don't want to.

> **Reflection Point**
> **Whose Agenda?**
>
> You have planned to carry out a painting activity with the babies.
>
> Let's set this up in two ways:
>
> A) Group activity paints are set up on the baby's tray and baby is sat in a highchair. Baby is stripped off to just a nappy. All begin.
>
> B) Baby is sat with practitioner on the covered floor, there is a large washable sheet and the paint is placed around. Practitioner shows the baby the paint and she explores it with her hand, describing to the baby what it feels like. Other baby becomes interested and smiles, he starts to touch the paint and the process of open-ended learning begins.

> What is our agenda? If the answer is to educate, then deep engagement in play at their own pace is crucial. Building brains is a repetitive and confidence-building pattern. No matter how tiny, we always seek out the baby's permission by watching out for and respectfully observing their cues and thoughts.
>
> Let's consider the role play area – this area is excellent for describing how things feel, letting the babies use objects and materials how they want (safely of course), and exploring different textures. You can think about the sounds that objects make and how they can be explored and played with in a number of ways.
>
> Lots of questions are not needed. Copying and mirroring what the babies do is great for allowing the baby to take the lead. They have the power at this moment, and it may surprise you how well they lead.

Messy Play

This area can be accessed at all times and is an ongoing process, using resources such as a covered palette, babies can continue to create and paint. Powder paint is fantastic for mixing and again that is part of being creative and messy. Now, this is a little contentious, however we are going to put it out there...aprons are not needed. Stopping a young child or baby in their flow of creativeness to put a 'plastic hard to move about in' apron on them really does not help. What does help is having lots of spare clothes to access after they have finished. We have seen amazing results in accessing creative and messy play when children are allowed to move freely and we know we are building brains, so reflect with your team and give it a go.

Smaller amounts of really interesting objects are brilliant to explore and create with, flowing materials that can be thrown up and floated down, gentle music on that can be painted to or danced to. Just a little note here, music on for a long time and as background does not help speech, as it can be difficult for the baby to filter out background noise and tune into the adult's voice, and it can also be too overwhelming.

A purpose for music and listening to different types of sounds adds another layer to creativeness. Babies can listen from 18 weeks in the womb so they are very practiced at tuning in. Discovering what they like unlocks another element of creativeness.

We know it is not working if the babies are disengaged and look fed up, if they are silently staring and just going through the motions. We want awe and wonder moments daily! Think about your best days out at the beach, what did you discover, how did it make you feel? That is what we want every day for babies' brain building. In fact, seaweed would be a great thing to explore!

Communication
What Would We Expect to See/Hear?

By six months:

- Babbling – making strings of sounds using a combination of vowels and consonants, for example 'dadada,' 'bababa'
- Still communicating their feelings/needs using different cries
- Respond by making noises when spoken to
- Smile at familiar faces

By 12 months:

- Vocalising along to songs
- Respond to their name by looking at the speaker
- Develop functional gestures such as waving and pointing
- May say a few single words
- Make sounds/vocalisations to get an adult's attention, and babble to people and toys
- Demonstrate understanding of words such as 'up' and 'bye bye'

By 18 months:

- Demonstrates understanding of simple questions such as 'where's Daddy?'
- May point to body parts on request
- May use ten or more words (might not say them clearly)
- Play develops – may start to play 'real-life' situations, for example making tea
- Copy new sounds/words

Vocabulary

Children at a vocalising/babbling stage need to hear you say and repeat single words. This is how they will learn their first words. Talk about what the baby is looking at or reaching for or playing with.

Use your outside environment to inspire you to 'teach' new vocabulary. Look around you, what can you see and hear?

> **Top Tip**
>
> It can be tempting to use baby talk with this age group and whilst it is natural to use 'motherese' – talking in a sing song voice, repeating ourselves, and using simple language, it is really important that we teach children the real word for what they are engaged with. We don't want to have to re-teach when the child gets older!

We are not expecting babies to demonstrate 'role play' – we know that is not developmentally appropriate, but they can experience a variety of materials and toys that they will later go on to play with and develop their imaginations. So, our role as the adult is to talk about the resources, and name the objects that the baby is exploring.

> **Top Tip**
>
> Remember that we must talk to babies! It sounds obvious but a baby will not learn their words if an adult does not speak to them. It can feel unnatural to comment on what baby is looking at or exploring using only single words but practise, practise, practise, and it will become easier and feel more natural.

Let's also consider the role of non-verbal communication for this age range! We need to look for eye pointing, which is a very subtle way that children show us what they're interested in or the more obvious, being taken by the hand and led to the object the child desires. It is so important that we add language to these situations, this is how children will learn.

We know that babies probably won't have the speech and language skills to make requests verbally but by interpreting their non-verbal communication, they are being heard and we are showing them that they matter to us!

Words, words, words! We've said it before and we will probably say it many times again throughout this book but we know that children need to hear words repeated many times for them to learn what that word means and how to use it.

Consider the words you're using. Messy/creative play gives us many rich, interesting words. We can comment using words such as 'splash' and 'squelch,' but we can also remember that for this age range, first speech sounds are likely to be 'p, b, t, d, m' – can we model single words that are loaded with these 'first sounds'?

> **Reflective Point**
>
> Think about the language you may find yourself using during messy/creative play.
>
> Can you think of words that contain those first 'speech sounds'?
>
> We need our language to be natural and relevant to what is happening for the baby but it is also possible to use this opportunity to model new vocabulary with target sounds.
>
> This sounds simple but it's not that easy in practice, take the time to have a practise!

Speech Sounds

We know that 'listening' is a skill that needs to be developed in children and it is a really important skill needed to learn speech sounds. Use your outside environment to introduce the baby to natural sounds. Comment on noises/sounds as you and baby hear them together – birds chirping, car horns beeping, aeroplanes, children's voices.

Babbling is a really important part of learning to talk – babies use this experience to experiment with sounds. They are also learning simple 'cause and effect,' *'when I make this sound, the grown up gets really excited and that makes me feel good.'*

We must notice when these babies are vocalising and babbling, they need us to respond and validate their efforts. Respond by smiling and celebrating and copy back the sound to the child. We are now introducing 'turn taking' – another really important skill for successful communication.

What natural sounds might we say as we explore 'role play resources'? Let's imagine we are exploring some fresh herbs with our babies, 'mmmmmm' would be a natural sound to make when we smell something interesting.

Think 'symbolic noises' – 'brmmmmmm' 'beep' – these will be sounds that naturally accompany toys and, with repetition, baby may make attempts to copy.

Messy/creative play gives us a great 'soundtrack.' Consider the sounds that you hear when you manipulate playdough, paint, or natural resources such as sand and mud. They all give us different sounds and we can talk about these sounds with our babies.

Copy the sounds you hear so that baby can experience the shared experience of listening to an interesting sound.

Modelling how to listen to these environmental sounds will support the babies in your care to develop this skill, so important for speech sound development.

The Role of the Educator – Adult-Child Interaction

Let's take a moment to reflect...

When do we interact?

What do we need to teach and how can we teach through natural play?

Interactions with babies and children are at their best when they are natural and invited. Practitioners and early educators hold so much power when working with young children, we must understand this and decide what we will do with this.

Using your place of influence to empower children by respecting them and what they are telling you (verbally or non-verbally) is key. What we are here to teach is confidence, independence, self-esteem, respect for others, and a lifelong desire to learn and be robust and resilient when we need to be. This is not created from the school of hard knocks; it is created from tuned-in educators and families who enable strong and secure attachments from which the baby can explore the world.

The outdoor environment can offer hours of natural wonder and free resources. The indoor environment is also great for snuggles and stories, music, and quality interactions. The main point here is that it is the time you give to build relationships, not the activities that are planned, which builds brains in babies.

We need to just mention sleep times. Now there are all sorts of ways babies like to sleep, and this needs to be reflected in their early years provisions. As adults we all go to sleep when we are tired and at different times, this is exactly the same for babies and young children. This is where flexible routines really matter.

Take a moment to think about the babies in your care. They may not yet be able to sit or may not be mobile, so think about your position. If the baby is lying down, join them – see the outside world from their perspective. If they are on their tummy, join them and establish a 'connection.' Show the baby you are interested in them by copying them and joining them in their outdoor experience.

Observe where they are looking or what engages them by observing what they track with their eyes. This gives you the opportunity to show them you are interested in them, name what they are looking at, or take them closer to what they are looking at.

> ### Reflection Point
>
> *A baby is unsure of an activity, they look to you for comfort and a cuddle.*
>
> *What do you do?*
>
> We know that everyone, and especially babies, learn better when they feel safe and that education is a process, **not** an end product. With this in mind, let's pick that baby up or get down to their level, let them snuggle in and talk to them gently about what is happening, and you tell them they are safe.
>
> The more the baby is comforted and understood, the sooner they will build connections in their brain, which then enable them to explore confidently.
>
> The more confidently they explore at their pace, the stronger their desire to learn will be.
>
> In a nutshell: be calm, be kind, be in the moment.

Deep Engagement in Play

We know that education is happening when children become deeply focused and engaged – by this we mean really concentrating, interacting, singing, or babbling to themselves or just a general demeanour of quiet pleasure.

They are playing with their own purpose and this is the time to let them be! Perhaps offer provocation by just placing another resource nearby (you don't need to draw their attention to it). Pathways in the baby brain are now being created. Wow! And to think that by reflecting on how you interact and providing resources, you have enabled a child's belief in their ideas!

Using imaginations to build up ideas and tapping into how the baby is playing, commenting on their play, and describing works so well. Lots of questions are not really needed. Copying and mirroring what the babies do is great for allowing the baby to take the lead. They have the power at this moment, and it may surprise you how well they lead.

Let the baby lead! We've said it before but it really matters. We often feel like our role as the adult is to teach but we need to know what the baby is interested in so that we can teach something that is meaningful to them.

Remember...children need a reason to communicate, motivation to communicate, and a responsive adult!

Be 'present,' be attentive but also know when to step back and let the baby explore.

Non-Verbal Communication

As a baby is exploring role play activities and toys, observe their eye gaze – where are they looking and what are they looking at? Can you copy their play? Are other babies showing interest by looking or reaching? Can you create a 'natural group' situation?

Quality interactions happen when the environment feels creative and not rushed. If a baby can't hold a paintbrush yet, then give them something they can hold (or better still allow them to explore); holding their hand and painting for them doesn't really engage a positive mindset, and diving into the paint with a fist or whole hand is another matter – however, again only if the baby wants to do this.

Some babies can be hesitant to start with, so respect this and model, put your hand in and describe what it feels like, reassure the baby that this is safe. Safe food products such as cornflour are a good place to start. Throughout creative play, whether this is expressive dancing and movement, singing, or exploring media and materials, the practitioner's role is always to support and not take over, to follow the baby's agenda not their own, to create confidence-giving environments where it is a positive experience to explore.

Observation is key here – when we take the time to really observe a baby's non-verbal communication, we may start to notice them looking towards other babies, they may reach out for other babies. This is our cue to add language to this very early interaction.

What might the baby be saying if they could speak?

'Hi Harry!' as baby looks towards his peer.

Yes, these babies may be very little but our role is to model how we interact, and introducing 'social language' at this stage is a good place to start.

Snack/Lunchtime

We have dedicated a whole section here to snack/lunchtime. This is something we do every day and it provides us with such a brilliant opportunity to really connect with a child, let's not allow it to be a missed opportunity for communication!

The Physical Environment

A calm physical environment is key. Think of your favourite time to eat – what is the atmosphere like? Why do you like it?

Eating can be a stressful time for many children and adults, there are all sorts of connotations connected to mealtimes, such as overfeeding, worrying about underfeeding, having to finish what is in front of you, having to say please and thank you before you are given food, having to wait too long to eat and then rushing. All of these have a negative effect on the child and the adult.

Think of the two things that children and babies can control: eating and going to the toilet, think of the two things that parents often want to know about: how much has my child eaten, have they been to the toilet today? Can you see a pattern emerging? The stress that is unwittingly caused and passed on to a baby can produce negative eating habits and create patterns for life. See, and we all thought it was just snack or lunchtime.

It is never just snack time or lunchtime, we are going to help you create a gorgeous, quality interactive way of ensuring the babies and children in your care thrive and love eating times. Let's continue on to the role of the educator.

The Role of the Educator – Adult-Child Interaction

Okay so we will dive straight in, you are the environment, you create the atmosphere, you decide if eating times will be awesome, calm, fun, and interactive. You decide if this time is valued, educational, two-way interactive, and enjoyable. You can give the power to the babies to gain confidence in eating for the rest of their life!

Wow, a lot of responsibility developing patterns in little human brains that will last the rest of their lives. Yes, it is a lot of responsibility! That is why we are going to help you to create the best environment possible in which to eat and learn.

How Can You Do This?

By observing, listening, and understanding. By creating your environment to mean that eating times really matter and are part of your in the moment and all planning aspects. By this we mean everything you create with the babies and children should have thought behind it; we don't mean it needs to be written down, it just needs to be discussed and understood.

> ## Reflection Point
>
> What happens now at eating times?
>
> Take just ten minutes to think about current routines and processes.
>
> **Key questions you might like to think about**
>
> Do you sit with the babies?
>
> Do you eat with them?
>
> Do you talk and listen together?
>
> Do you and your colleagues interact naturally around the babies and include them in conversations
>
> Do you follow their lead and comment on their conversations – babbling, gestures, pointing – are you interested in what they have to say?
>
> **Key Reflection Point**
>
> Everything you do is educational – so even if it's not intentional, the baby will learn from you.
>
> Written planning is only one element of learning – babies learn from the natural quality interactions you have with them, this can be observed and written up afterwards if needed. The next steps are natural next steps, knowing the baby really well is so much better than writing about a baby.
>
> Your practice and life will be enhanced through eating times being relaxed, unhurried, and part of your in the moment planning.

Families and Eating

Sharing how babies eat when they are in your care is crucial, however it's not what they have eaten, or the amount, even though we all like to know our babies eat. Remember that we are trusting babies and children, they will eat when they are hungry.

Babies have an automatic shut-off when they are full, by repeatedly overriding this we are not helping them to regulate for the future, and we are changing key innate natural eating habits. Our stomachs tell our brains when we are full, we just need to listen. Babies also know when they are hungry and this might not fit in with other babies – fair enough really, we all get hungry at different times.

A baby waiting too long for food can create patterns of eating very quickly and gulping food, causing uncomfortable stomach aches and not tasting food; this may also lead to overeating. This is why there is a need for flexible baby-driven routines, if you are thinking this doesn't fit in with your routine or practice there is some help on developing this idea further.

Please see Chapter 4 for more discussion on routines.

Eating times are not rushed, highly structured, or let's get this done times. Be honest and talk with your colleagues if it feels like this, the good thing is you now have the support and opportunity to change and create a positive experience for everyone.

Babies are much more likely to eat in a relaxed environment where they are valued and understood. We want babies to eat to thrive because it is what their body needs, babies who are stressed may create patterns of emotional eating which could last a lifetime. What is needed is calm, enjoyment, and time to experiment with food with a tuned-in adult for support when needed.

When a baby has finished eating they can help to wipe themselves and get down and play, waiting for another baby or child to finish will only cause frustration at this young age. One fair rule here, food is eaten at the table, not while walking around. So if a young child gets up that is fine, they can even return; however, food stays on the table. This can be done calmly, 'food at the table please,' 'if you want to play that's ok.' Now we know what you are thinking, this might not work in practice; however, it really does – after a little while the children know that they are trusted and the novelty of getting up soon goes.

This also means children who eat very slowly are not rushed, they can carry on eating and observe others happily. See now you have a completely satisfied and trusted, unhurried eating time. You are listening to everyone's needs and more importantly you are hearing them. You are on an even stance and the baby sees you as a trusted conversation partner. Fantastic teaching well done!

Eating times should feel like you are teaching positive habits for a lifetime of love of food; remember compassionate teaching is needed in every aspect of your practice, you are responsible for creating a community of lifelong learners. In this case, you will have taught the baby that eating is an enjoyable, positive, and constructive time to talk, listen, and be heard. In a nutshell, you are telling the babies that they matter – remember this is a fundamental human need for all humans to thrive.

We interact naturally in conversation with serve and return, waiting for pauses as you would as if you were chatting with your friend. Be mindful of when the babies turn away, this is when they are interacting and then stop and almost seem to daydream or look away, this is a time for quiet from their interactive adult. This signals the baby is processing and connections are being strengthened in their brain and this is actual brain building. The baby will then usually resume play or move on.

Do you see the importance of your role and the value you bring to a child's life by just being in the moment, observing their cues, and respecting their ideas? Quality interactions happen when you are present in the moment, this applies to eating times and the experience that is given to each child.

Remembering that practice is built upon daily, so what worked yesterday at lunchtime might not work today. A child might love cheese one day and not touch it the next, this is a child processing, testing out their ideas, and seeing what response they are given. Eating like all education is a process and not an end result.

We have offered cheese...the child does not want it today.

As a practitioner do we:

- Comment?
- Leave cheese on the table in reach?
- Take the cheese away?

Any one of the above is fine if it is carried out in a positive, interactive teaching manner with good body language.

Our body language is extremely easy to read and babies are experts at understanding what is happening, that is how they survive.

A positive way forward for all meals is to give a choice so the babies can help themselves and explore with their senses – touching, smelling, and tasting. The calmer we are the calmer the baby will be.

Babies in this age range are highly dependent on the adults to get their food and to eat safely; this is great because it means they have the adult's full attention.

This is a brilliant opportunity to be 'present' with the baby, sit at their level, and engage them with social smiles and eye contact.

We know that children learn through imitation and how many of us open our mouth as we approach a baby's mouth with a spoon?

Enjoy this experience and take the time to remember it is not just about getting a baby fed, this is a prime social experience and we must not miss the opportunity to engage and communicate.

Communication
Vocabulary Boost

This is a really good opportunity for teaching words; we are surrounded by first words during snack and lunchtime. We can use the opportunity to name food, drink, cup, bowl, spoon, table. At this stage children will start to develop their first words and these will typically be nouns (objects).

> **Top Tip**
>
> Remember we need to name the object that the child is engaged with, this is how they will learn and repeat, repeat, repeat!

Speech Sound Boost

How can the development of weaning and eating link with speech sound development? Let's think about the mechanics of eating... At around six to nine months, a baby has learnt to clean a spoon with their upper lip. This is an important development of upper lip muscles, which will be essential for developing the speech sounds 'm,' 'b,' and 'p' (sounds produced by bringing both lips together).

At around nine to 12 months, a baby demonstrates lip closure while swallowing liquids and soft solids. Often this is the stage where we hear babble and this ability to achieve lip closure will be a skill essential for developing speech sounds and reduplicated babble (strings of repeated sounds, ma ma, ba, ba, ba).

The baby is beginning to experiment with drinking liquids from a sippy cup, this promotes lip rounding, which will be essential for speech sound development (vowels and bilabial sounds – sounds produced using both lips).

So you can see how the development of muscles used for eating has a strong link to speech sound development. Be mindful during this activity that it is not just about feeding the child, there is much learning to be done here.

Speech, Language, and Communication Needs

When/how would we know if a child was struggling with their communication?

Children at this age are 'explorers,' as they begin to gain independence with their physical skills their world opens up to new experiences and opportunities.

Look

- Does the child explore the environment and the toys available?
- Is the child showing an awareness (watching, copying, following) of the adults and the other children?
- Does the child smile and show 'enjoyment' when you interact with them?
- Does the child react to sounds/noises by turning their body/head towards the sound?
- Does the child have any difficulty eating and/or drinking?

Listen

- Is the child making any sounds/babbling or are they quiet?

Learn

If you are concerned about any of the above talk to the child's parents/carers. Children who are struggling to explore toys have reduced opportunities to hear adults teaching them new vocabulary. They have fewer opportunities to explore toys and gain an understanding of cause and effect and that they have an influence on their environment by 'making things happen.'

Communication is a social act and if a child is not responding when you interact with them they will not have the opportunity to learn the social aspects of communication – smiling, eye contact, body language, and early turn-taking.

If a child is not visibly responding to sound, do they need to have a hearing test? Hearing and speech go hand in hand so we need to ensure that children can hear us.

Eating and drinking difficulties can be serious – if a child is coughing and choking then they need to be assessed by a specialist speech and language therapist.

It is important that we discuss our concerns but it is vital that we don't diagnose.

Remember – *discuss, don't diagnose!*

At this stage we need to share our observations with parents/carers; they may have made similar observations themselves but it is possible that you may be presenting new information to them about their child and this may be upsetting to hear.

Be sensitive in your approach but be clear about what you have observed and why you are sharing it with them.

HOW CAN WE SUPPORT THE CHILD WITH SPEECH, LANGUAGE, AND COMMUNICATION NEEDS?

Practitioner Toolkit

- ❖ Opportunity
- ❖ Interaction
- ❖ Respond-repeat

Opportunity

Ensure children have access to toys which are motivating and interesting to the child. Consider those children who are not yet mobile, ensure they have the **opportunity** to explore.

If you have observed that the child is not engaging with their environment, observe their non-verbal communication. Where are they looking? What are they reaching for? Can you interpret that non-verbal communication and provide **opportunities** to engage?

Interaction

Be available but also give space to explore.

If the child is not responding to adults' or other children's attempts to engage, then it is really important that you are sensitive with your **interactions**. You will need to observe what the child is doing and gently position yourself alongside the child. Copying what the child is doing shows the child that you are interested in them and how they play. Notice if the child stops what they are doing or if they look towards you, pause and see what happens next. Does the child give you a cue (eye contact, body movement, vocalisation) that they want you to carry on doing what you were doing?

Respond-Repeat

We have referred to this strategy before but remember it is really important at this stage of development that we **respond** to the children's communicative attempts. The child may still be at the babbling/making sounds stage (stage 2 – see Chapter 1), and we can still **respond** and **repeat**. By **repeating** back the sounds that the child is making, we are showing the child that we are interested in them and we 'get them.' We can also extend their sounds into words – if the child is playing with a ball and babbling the sounds 'ba, ba, ba,' we **respond** and model 'ball.'

For target suggestions and interventions, see Chapter 8.

4
18 MONTHS TO TWO YEARS

18 months to two years – we are no longer working with young babies, however the children are still very new to the world. This is another very amazing period of growth and development, especially in physical and communication skills. During this period, we are expecting to hear those exciting first words and possibly even short phrases. We will often see children testing their own physical capabilities by climbing and taking more risks as they grow their awareness of their physical self.

As with every stage of development, we have an active role in supporting children's development and with light touch teaching, you can offer intrigue and challenge which will enhance the child's learning and experiences.

Play and the Environment

The physical environment – Let's take a moment to reflect...

What does the environment look like?

Children from 18 months will need choice, we want to encourage them to explore widely and through different terrains. Exploring and becoming an adventurer is crucial for children to thrive and have brighter futures. Have a think about the following: is there opportunity for children to explore different mediums? Do they have mud, sand, water, playdough, paints on offer? *Can they really choose resources to explore?* Activities that are 'set up' can have a place, however we believe this doesn't have to be the norm. Deep engagement in play comes from listening and observing a child, letting them lead and choose what they want to do. You then extend when the time is right, 'I noticed that you like...' or 'I saw this and thought of you.' Keeping children in mind enables self-confidence because they know they matter to you and that you understand them.

We are huge advocates of free flow, by this we mean an area of outside and inside from which children can choose for much of the time. This is crucial in helping children to build the physical and social skills they need to thrive. Adults must also remember that the child knows who they are and what they like. You have the power to give them the respect they deserve; they will then be enabled to build upon this and become independent in their physical environment.

Can children use their senses to explore, what smells can they smell? Do you explore new smells such as coffee, tea, herbs, flowers, are there safe plants that children can use in their mixtures? Is your environment truly inspirational, do you go into it and think 'wow, I am building brains right here right now?' Or do you think 'mmm this is a bit boring.' Perhaps you think 'I would love to be a toddler here' or 'there is not a chance I would want to be here as a child.' This is where you need to be totally honest!

Is it working, and how do we know it is working?

The first question you will need to ask is, what does it feel like to enter this room? Do the children look engaged (really interested in what they are doing)? Are the children laughing, smiling, thinking, playing, and are all children catered for? Is there a child who has body language that tells you they are just going through the motions? Eighteen months to two-year-old environments can be very overlooked. In some early years environments, it can seem like a bit of a toddler transition phase. Is your environment working? Let's read on and discover the importance of how to find the answer to this crucial question. The following template may help you and your team to reflect, change, question, and expand your physical environment. Remember everyone should be involved in understanding their physical presence in the environment, this has a huge role to play in early years.

Everyday practice is to constantly reflect and see what purpose our resources have, what do they offer for our toddlers and why are they there? Are the resources extended and what provocation is there to build young children's brain development and language skills? It isn't enough to have a resource that looks good or is quite popular, as early years professionals we need to observe and discover why and what next. For a positive physical environment, the quality of the team's interactions, comments, and extension of play is the key element. This age group of children will give you many clues through their communication (verbal or non-verbal), and it is for us to interact, notice, and become intrigued in giving children the very best start.

Reflection Point

We all know what it feels like when someone really 'gets us,' your confidence grows when you and your ideas are actively listened to and understood. This is the foundation of great communication. To create an environment where young children can thrive, you will need to be that person who actively listens, understands, and builds confidence. Your physical presence in noticing and commenting on what you see is paramount. Being in the moment and being present is the skill that all great teachers require.

Remember we are all always learning, so what may have worked before might not work now. Embrace change as it brings great opportunity for teaching and learning for everyone. This template is for extending ideas and thoughts and is not a tick sheet. Talk with your colleagues, write all over it, and use it to create brighter futures and confidence in young children and the teams that work with them.

Environmental Reflection 18–24 Months: Is It Working, and How Do We Know It Is Working?

Reflection and talking points	Why? Questioning ideas, practice, and routines helps us understand the physical environment and what it is like to be a toddler in your setting. Here are some practical ways of assessing your physical environment.	Yes The adults think this works well for now and know why it works well.	No or not sure The adults think we need to spend a little time to understand this and we will try a different idea/approach and then reflect upon this.
What does the room feel like?	Walk in and what do you feel? Ask the children, ask older children.		
What does the room smell like?	Actually smell the room and ask others what does this smell evoke? *Be mindful of children who are more sensitive to smell – we may think the lavender smells good but for some children this can be too stimulating and lead to distraction and even distress.*		
Are there resources that children are allowed to choose and explore when they want to?	Can children choose throughout their day and move resources around to extend their play and ideas? *Example: What happens if a toddler picks up a paint bottle and wants to paint?*		
How do adults extend children's learning naturally?	How much do adults understand how each individual child learns and plays?		
Are children heard?	Are children's ideas, thoughts, concerns, emotions validated however they communicate (non-verbal or verbal)? *NB: Toddlers are often communicating non-verbally and we can learn so much from this.*		
Are children's emotions talked about in everyday practice? If so, how?	Example: a child is sad, is this recognised and vocalised 'Sophie, you seem sad,' 'Sam, you look worried.'		
Is every child understood?	How do we know this? How well do we know each child (what is their life story so far)?		
Is there a person who comes into the room and the atmosphere changes?	All adults have the power to transform a room. This can have a negative effect, positive effect, calming effect, exciting effect. Have a think as a team and be honest – what happens when you each walk in the room?		
Does every adult understand the power of their physical presence in the room?	Some points you might like to think about: How do adults position themselves? What is their body language like? How do they communicate?		

Copyright material from Poulter Jewson and Skinner (2022), *Speech and Language in the Early Years: Creating Language-Rich Learning Environments*, Speechmark

18 Months to Two Years

Does the environment feel fair?	Are everyone's needs catered for? Are the rules fair and kind? Do situations escalate quickly? Do the adults hold all the power and do children have choice and are they involved in decision making (remember to watch for non-verbal in this age group)?		
Does the environment feel fun, do children smile a lot?	Are all children pleased to be with you and the other adults? How do you know?		
Can children engage and play and extend their ideas?	Are adults receptive to children's communication and do they keep their word? *Example: 'We could have a look together at making an aeroplane after lunch,'* *'I am just talking with Zeya and then I can listen to your idea.'*		
Free-flow – can children choose to be inside or outside? In this case we mean: Playing with the doors open and interacting between both inside and outside environments, naturally engaging and playing. Adults extend and engage through really knowing and understanding the child, their interests, and their patterns of play.	There is more information on free-flow throughout the book. As you know we are advocates for play where children deeply engage and their communications are highly valued.		
How many adults like inside best? Do we know why this is?	Be honest! All people have environments they prefer and thrive in. When we understand and explore this we can work well and enable full potential (yours and the children's).		
How many adults like outside best? Do we know why this is?	Be honest! All people have environments they prefer and thrive in. When we understand and explore this we can work well and enable full potential (yours and the children's).		
Do young children have access to a story they choose – can this be read or played with just by children who are interested?	Can this happen in the moment? If not possible straight away how can you keep the child in mind and go back to this?		
Do all the 18–24-month-aged children have to join in together for certain activities? How long is this for?	Question why the children are brought together. Does this hinder play? Are expectations of children too high? Are children deeply engaged (brain development) or are they just conforming? Is this the time that children get upset or frustrated? How could you do this differently? *NB: Remember our role is to support, nurture, and teach, we do this by understanding brain development in young children.*		

Copyright material from Poulter Jewson and Skinner (2022), *Speech and Language in the Early Years: Creating Language-Rich Learning Environments*, Speechmark

Is there a cosy sofa (like a lounge at home) where adults and children can snuggle and relax together? Or where children and their friends can chat together undisturbed?	This can be a sofa that has been donated or a few comfy chairs, this reflects real life and creates a caring, relaxed environment that welcomes you in. This is not about spending lots of money and creating a special unused area; rather, use it and let children explore and feel at home. **Reflection Point:** It is only in childcare settings where everything is tiny; homes and real life are not like this. So have a think what you really need?		
What happens if a child hits out or bites?	Is the adult response measured and calm? Do adults understand that children of 18–24 months cannot 'think why they did this.' Is there a caring and learning outcome? Are adults consistent? What did the children learn from this? When is it the right time to look at actions of the child? How do you role model empathy? How do you teach theory of mind (understanding our actions affect others, putting ourselves in others' space)? Do all adults ensure that children are not 'shamed' or singled out for their actions?		
How do adults speak to children?	Does this make everyone feel relaxed, understood, and supported?		
Are children often crying?	All adults need to understand and validate emotions as this is vital for robust mental health and positive teaching environments.		
Do you have somewhere to eat that looks like you would want to eat there? Are children involved with the process of lunch? What is the learning outcome of your eating times?	One idea that we have used successfully is an old kitchen table (donated). If children are using highchairs this works as a family mealtime and you are an extension of the children's families. Think...if children are with you all day what is their experience of eating? If they are able to they can sit on chairs up to the table with you. Eat with the children – this is what happens in real life!		

18 Months to Two Years

You can use this table to reflect on what is working and what is not. When you work with toddlers the room you are in can sometimes become overwhelming and cluttered. Young children often like to transport or empty toys, this is a key element of their development and ensuring you understand what each child likes to do then means you can build upon this. Try to bring in new objects for the toddlers to explore, show them many different media, such as clay, mud, grass, rocks, pebbles, and seaweed. Keep thinking about extending understanding of the natural resources around you. You are working with a brilliant age group who are experiencing many 'firsts' in their lives! You are visibly teaching them, do not let your toddler room become the in-between room where they are not babies and not pre-schools. Use this precious time to teach naturally and find out who these children are and what they love to do. This is not about setting up activities, it is about having interesting resources throughout your play environment and the key element is you and your team knowing when and how to comment and communicate with the children.

> ### Reflection Point
> **Whose Agenda? 18–24 Months**
>
> You have planned to carry out a storytime (this could also apply to circle time).
>
> Let's set this up in two ways:
>
> A) Group activity – the chairs or cushions are set up around you. You sit on a surface higher than the children. You choose a book, and say, 'everyone sit down and let's begin.'
>
> B) A toddler shows interest in a book or story, you notice that they look at it and then look at you. Practitioner smiles and comments, 'we could look at the book together.' The child responds, smiles, nods or shakes their head, or sometimes does nothing. The practitioner talks about the story and the child relaxes and opens the book. The child skips a couple of pages and then stays on one page, the practitioner comments on what they see and uses positive body language, and then the process of open-ended learning begins. Another child may come and join in or just have a look. The child then may choose to look at the same book repeatedly, this is all part of brain development for the young child.
>
> A few more points to consider:
>
> - ❖ Body positioning – you can snuggle if the child wants to or just be near each other.
> - ❖ Be at the child's level.
> - ❖ If many children want to join in and there is space, then great, let them.

- ❖ If many children want to join in and there is no space, either move to a bigger space if possible or ask another adult to look at books with other children.
- ❖ The child who chooses the book has ownership of it until they have finished with it or discarded it. If another child wants the book they will need to have another book or wait (obviously this is put in place kindly).

Sharing for young children, now here is a hot topic! If you were working on your laptop and someone came and took it, what might you say? It would be surprising if you did not say anything, and you just let them have it. Let's take this scenario a little deeper, you say to your friend that someone has just taken your laptop and you were in the middle of using it and they reply, 'it's nice to share, sharing is caring.' Now what would you feel like saying and doing? We must apply how we feel as adults and the power we have in our lives to that of young children. Children will learn to share and will develop theory of mind when they are shown kindness and modelled behaviour from adults.

If another child takes their toy or changes their game and what they learn is that this child is enabled to do this, then they will also do this. We now have a scenario where when a child wants something they just tell an adult and get it, another child's deep engagement in play is changed and the outcome is often negative.

So how do we create positive communication around sharing? We talk with children and vocalise what is happening, we have more of the same resources, for example, making lots of playdough so there is enough for everyone. Yes, children do need to learn to take turns and wait, this is often carried out with sand timers and visual clues. They need responsive adults to help contain their disappointment when their turn has finished. Children need fair and consistent boundaries that they understand; they may become upset, however you will support them and explain that you know it's disappointing or frustrating for them and that they will have another turn. Turn-taking at this age is about building foundations and supporting emotions and not having huge expectations. Sharing can often be mis-interpreted as a child being 'selfish' or 'naughty' or just not listening and this is not the case, they are just engaged in the moment and with that toy.

As adults we do not always see the full picture and it is good to look at what happened before and after a sharing incident. Respond kindly and do not react. Encourage the child to come up with an answer and help work out how to find solutions to sharing and turn-taking problems that occur. Obviously, this needs help and supportive adults to embed this in practice, then it becomes the norm that children try to work out solutions. It really is one of the best moments in practice when you observe this problem-solving communication and sustained shared thinking that you have helped to create. This is a great life skill and starts with supportive adults who understand child development.

18 Months to Two Years

A Quick Case Study: Supporting Sharing and Turn-Taking 18–24 Months

Jimmy is playing with the train set and has four of the trains, he is chatting to himself and is deeply engaged on his own. Petal comes along and would like to play with the train set, there is plenty of spare track and she starts to build and connect the track with the help of an adult. After a little while she spots Jimmy as he pushes his trains around the track; she wants one and goes to take it. Jimmy shouts 'no train,' Petal gets upset and cries, then starts breaking up the track.

What could the practitioner's response be?

What do you think you might do?

- Think about how you would respond; what would your tone of voice be?
- Who would you comfort first?
- What would you do to help the situation to calm?
- What natural teaching moments could you support?
- What would the children learn from this situation?
- How smoothly do you feel you and the adults around you would respond to this situation?
- Would all communication responses from adults be consistent?

Thinking about how to respond: Petal seems like she would need a cuddle or some comforting words because she is crying and is cross. Jimmy has been playing quite happily and for his age and stage development has told Petal not to take his trains. The adult could help Petal to rebuild the track or simply ask Jimmy if he wanted to rebuild it, depending on how upset Jimmy becomes about it.

In this situation the adult might say, 'let's sort this out together, Petal you look sad and cross, Jimmy you sounded cross.' As you say this your body language would be calm and you are starting to help both children self-regulate through co-regulating them (lending them some of your calmness). You could start to help mend the track and find Petal some trains, commenting, 'Jimmy has those trains, you could use these, Petal.' You could comment to Jimmy, 'Petal liked your game and would like to play by you.' Jimmy and Petal within this age group of 18–24 months are not old enough to understand that their actions affect each other. As the professional and the adult, you can support and teach them by commenting, 'Petal you look sad,' 'Jimmy you had a loud voice,' 'I think it frightened Petal.' The children do not need to look at you to hear and they do not need to acknowledge you, they will hear you and they will be influenced by your response. Once it is calm you could comment positively and say something along the lines of 'It is so lovely when you are playing kindly.'

Young children will experience many emotions and it is for the adults in their lives to support these and teach them. A word of caution – never ask young children to sit out and think about what they have done, they do not have the capacity to do this and you will bring negative attention into the mix. Young children do not need to say sorry; they do not know what this means, and they will say it to please you and to move on. We have all observed children who hit another child and immediately say sorry and then do it again. You can model empathy by calmly saying, 'look Marley is sad, that hurt him, what could we do to make him feel better?' The adult could suggest perhaps a cuddle, a favourite toy or book, show the children empathy in practice. Ask the child who is upset, 'what can we do to make you feel better?' Never shame a child by repeating loudly what they have done to other team members. Shaming children and calling them out or making them sit out or shouting at them will not help their confidence or self-esteem and does not help child development.

Communication
What Would We Expect to See/Hear?

By two years:

- ❖ Understand simple instructions such as 'get your shoes'
- ❖ Use about 50 words (may still not be clear)
- ❖ Repeat words they hear
- ❖ Start to combine words to form little sentences such as 'Daddy gone'

How are you talking and communicating with the children?

Do you feel like the people you work with communicate well with children?

Do you feel like it would be great to understand more about young children's communication?

We love to observe young children knowing that we can be part of the reason that they thrive and they then go on to role model their fabulous communication skills to others. Early years are about building positive communication for the future. The children you work with now are very young and you have the skills to help them build their best possible lives!

Communication is the foundation of all great teaching. Listening to and observing children's communication in play is a vital skill for adults working in early years. When observing this age group, you need to discover how each individual child is communicating; this means giving them the space to play, interact and be themselves. It also means picking up on cues that the child sends out to you. This could be as subtle as a look, a nod, a glance, their fingers going into their mouth, them twirling their hair, the child avoiding eye contact and looking away, their eyes becoming a little sad, and them looking unsure. Now the list is not exhaustive, however it gives you a few clues as to the very subtle behaviours young children use to communicate with us; your power is in observing these and showing the child that their communication is important to you. Developing confidence in this way enables the child to thrive and build upon their ideas and thoughts. They begin to show and develop their personality and know that being themselves is great. They know this because you have taught them that however they choose to communicate you will try to understand them.

Positive brain development does not just happen – quality interactions are vital for strengthening pathways in a child's brain. Young children are programmed to seek relationships and they need the adults in their life to interact and communicate with them warmly and with positive body language. Basically, they need you to like them and show them that they matter and they are worth listening to. They need you to help them when they feel overwhelmed and upset, they want you to have fun with them and to be consistent. Young children build resilience by being shown that their emotions can be supported by caring adults. You are teaching them that it is alright to communicate that they are sad, happy, worried, and to know that when they show their emotions they will be supported by a calm, clear response with kindness and co-regulation.

Vocabulary

At this stage, children can have a significant boost in their vocabulary. We know that children will typically understand more words than they can say and the role of the adult here is to continue 'teaching' new words.

When learning first words and first phrases, children will typically learn words which are useful to them, this is because in order to become successful communicators children need to be motivated to communicate – they need a reason! This may be to show you something, to make a request, or to refuse. Just be mindful that when children are developing first words and phrases, concepts such as colours and numbers may be interesting but are not especially functional to the young child here. When we are 'teaching' vocabulary through natural, play- based interactions it is more useful for the child to learn the name of the object they are exploring rather than the colour. There is a time and place for teaching colours but consider the child you are interacting with – which word will be more useful to them? A child who is yet to develop any spoken words will benefit more from hearing the name of the object he is playing with repeated and modelled to him so that as he develops his words, he can then request 'car' rather than 'red' if he can't find the desired 'red car.'

The child who is developing phrases would benefit from new concepts such as colour to help them to put words together but remember there are other words that we can use, not just colours – consider 'fast car,' 'car driving,' 'Daddy's car,' 'car up,' 'car down' – so many options.

> **Top Tip**
>
> Watch and wait...and then join in! Watch how the child tells you things – remember this may not be with words so you really do need to practice the watch and wait strategy. Watch how the child tells you things and then add the words.

Speech Sounds

At this stage children are still experimenting with speech sounds. We would not expect words to be clear as the child is still learning how to produce sounds and how to combine them into recognisable words.

Let's remember that some children at this stage may still be babbling and not yet be saying any words.

Listening skills continue to develop throughout this stage. We need to be aware of the sounds and noise level of the learning environment. Music and songs are great and are beneficial for communication development but be careful if using music as background noise. Children need time to develop listening skills and this includes being able to filter out certain sounds/noise in order to focus on other things – adults talking for example. We can make this easier for the child by just being aware of background noise and reduce where possible.

So, music and singing – how can this support speech sound development?

Nursery rhymes are typically very repetitive, providing the child with the opportunity to hear words over and over again. This supports vocabulary development but also provides an opportunity to practice saying the words. The rhyming element of these songs is an early introduction to the world of phonological awareness. Phonological awareness refers to an understanding that sets of sounds combine together to make words and requires knowledge of rhyme and syllable awareness as well as the ability to hear and then produce the beginning and end of words.

Are we comfortable singing in front of people?

Children don't need us to sing to a professional standard but they do need to experience the rhyme, rhythm, and repetition that songs provide, and for this to be accessible to their developing attention and listening skills, the adults need to be confident, slow, and clear when they sing. Use of visual props can enable this experience to be more meaningful for children. Please be mindful of the pace of your singing – children need time to listen, process, and then join in; they will only be able to do this successfully if the adult is going at a steady pace.

Songs with actions provide an opportunity for children who do not yet have their words to join in and feel a part of their community.

The Role of the Educator – Adult-Child Interaction

Very simply, the children need to know that they matter to you, that your response will be consistently kind, and that they can relax and play. When a child relaxes their brain develops, when a child is nervous or hypervigilant because they do not know how their caregiver or educator will respond then they cannot learn. All adults who work with young children must know and understand how to communicate with children.

Children need adults around them who love them; this is no different because the adults around them are paid. There is no difference in a child's mind: you are part of their extended family and this role must be taken with the huge amount of respect it deserves. We are privileged to work with young children and shape their lives and brains. Adults build futures every minute of the day they work with children.

All the children will notice and know how the adults respond to them and the other children, so if there is one child who is often singled out or a child who is not noticed, the other children will be affected by this. If there is one shouty adult in your practice then this needs to be addressed. The ethos of practice must be one that has child development and communication at the heart of it. As adults working with young children, it is our duty to protect and nurture every single child.

Young children will require the adults in their lives to observe them and extend their interest and play ideas naturally, to have fun and laugh with them, to cuddle them when they are upset, to know about and understand child development, to contain their emotions and name these for them, to respond calmly and to be their cheerleader and want the best for them, to know them so well and to pass on this knowledge as the child grows and moves on to other classrooms or settings. At times young children will need you to be their voice when things aren't going well in their lives, to speak up for them and ensure that they have been heard.

Routines

We have dedicated a whole section here to routines. Routines can be important, however they can also be limiting. There are many times of the day when we are transitioning or preparing for what is coming next and it can be easy to get absorbed in this and miss the 'teaching moment' or the child's subtle or not-so-subtle cue. Let's not allow routines to be a barrier to communication and quality interaction.

Is your routine flexible? Can it change and do you and the adults in the environment reflect on your routine? We know how busy early years are and sometimes standing back and reflecting seems impossible. So, we are here to help. Flexible routines will enhance everyone's life in your setting and it will free up time to be in the moment and understand what young children need.

When we work with children we must always look at 'why' and what is happening for them right now. Why do we have circle time? Why do we have snack time? Why are the children allowed outside only at certain times? Why are they allowed to paint on Tuesday but not on Thursday? You get the gist – often routines are in place that do not support the child's confidence, pace of play, and deep engagement.

What is a flexible routine? That really is down to which children are with you and how much you know about each and every one of them. We can give you the fundamentals of the flexible routine and then teams can reflect on this and what this means for the children in the setting. This doesn't mean all changes you put in place will work and often people are afraid of changing things. It's good to think 'what is the worst that can happen here?' If you make changes and everyone hates it, change it back. You will still have reflected, discussed, and discovered what the adults in the team need to understand to embrace change. You will have also looked at how children actually learn and have a greater understanding of deeper engagement in play.

The Physical Environment and Routines

If you learn from a young age that your communications matter, then you will have the skills needed to interact with others, treasure communications, and most importantly be able to listen and observe. You will know that however you communicate you are heard and will feel a valued member of your community, which we hope is a feeling that continues to develop and grow. All this comes from being heard, understood, and valued in early years and education. See how important you are as an adult in a young child's world, we cannot say it enough: *You hold the key to brighter futures*!

Ensuring young children are involved in their routines is key. With the toddlers there will be a fair amount of routine to their day. A young child's routine may become quite rigid, and as early years educators and adults in the child's life, it is key that we ensure routines are flexible and as calm as possible; we also want to have some fun, which is often overlooked.

What are the main things a young child might have in their routine in a day? Sleeping, eating, nappy changing, teeth cleaning, nap time, songs and story, playtime, playdates, toddler clubs, visits to friends and family, outings. We are sure you can think of many more things, so how do you get the balance right?

You could use this template as a guide to help you get started.

Flexible routine *What happens throughout the day*	*Opportunities for child development and teaching moments in a flexible routine with child development at the core*
Examples: *Nappy changing times* Key communication time: Your professional time is for the child not just the routine of nappy changing. If it feels rushed to the adult, how does the child feel? Asking permission: How do you ask the child to come and have their nappy changed? This is all part of the respectful teaching and learning moments, do not let the routine get in the way of respecting the child. **Reflection Point:** What would you feel like if you were a child in your nappy changing process?	Are these when the child needs changing? Are these at a certain time every day? Are these times used to: • Talk with the child • Tell them what's happening • Connect with them • Sing with them • Ensure each individual child has time and respect. We are not talking massive amounts of time, we are understanding the power of meaningful interactions in every aspect of your work and the child's life.

Flexible routine What happens throughout the day	Opportunities for child development and teaching moments in a flexible routine with child development at the core
Changing out of wet clothes Putting on coats and shoes	What do we want the child to learn? Here is a great opportunity to build independent skills and teach about buttons, zips, Velcro, to build 'I can' attitudes. Again, this is a great skill, and if we are thinking about school readiness then children going to school able to get changed for PE or put their coat on themselves is great – they will be the first one out in the playground to run wild and free. They will build on their independent skills. Young children like to share skills and help each other, encouraging this at clothes changing times works well for building emotional and social skills. **Reflection Point:** Remember this is a teaching and learning connection moment, not a mad rush where all of us get ready at the same time. If you know a child takes longer, then give them more time, ask them to get ready a bit sooner, and give them help where needed. We learn from being supported, encouraged, and helped where needed. Question why do you all go out at the same time: Can you go out at staggered times when the faster children are ready? Keeping children waiting and all gathered together does not add to teaching and learning.
Home time – make it a good transition	There can be a high level of tiredness by this time (children and adults) and children can be listening for doorbells and may be on high alert. Having relaxing areas where children can snuggle or finish off their play ideas works well. Having a big storytime doesn't always work as it is just passing the time. Enabling children to play and carry on as usual is key to helping their transitions. Adults can certainly communicate calmly that it is nearly time to go home and children can help to get ready.
Eating times	Consider when this is and can it be offered once children have had a big chunk of play? **Reflection Point:** How many minutes can a young child sit for? Roughly about the same as how old they are. How long have they been asked to sit, were they sitting before they came to eat? How involved are they in preparation? Are adults sitting with children? Can children leave the table once they have finished and engage straight back into play? Eating at a young age is more of an inconvenience so it is up to the adults to make it chatty and fun. Look at the expectations the adults have for children and adjust accordingly. NB: Young children often have little power in their lives and eating or not eating is one of them, tread very carefully and never ask young children to eat once they have finished or eat up so that they have a treat after, we are creating brain patterns for life. It is important that we reflect on our teaching methods.

Flexible routine What happens throughout the day	Opportunities for child development and teaching moments in a flexible routine with child development at the core
Starting times You set the atmosphere and physical and emotional environment from this moment of the child's day.	**The Adults** The best way to start the day is with a relaxed adult who cares. If you come to work and are stressed, then you need to take some time and speak with your colleagues. If you work alone then look at your routine and try to make things a little easier and more flexible. Find networks of support and book yourself a supervision. We must be honest about how we feel and understand and value our own emotions, then we can teach to the best of our ability. **The Children** The children could come in and self-register, put bags where they need to go (younger children may need some help with this). Adults will have recorded the time they arrive. The adult welcomes each child as they come in and the child goes off to play, has a cuddle, or does whatever they need to do to settle.
Playtime Extended periods of time where children are deeply engaged	Give long periods of time where children can test their ideas and thoughts, add resources nearby, and comment where invited or you can naturally extend. Children have amazing ideas, trust them, let them have their childhood and build upon these. Observe and wait to be invited, look for the cues and gestures.
Outdoor time Can this be offered throughout the whole day?	Offer inside and outside for most of the time, trust children to know where they want to play and embrace outside. If you cannot create access to both areas, how can you enable outside to be natural and used as much as possible for longer, more frequent periods of time?
Circle time Do the children genuinely love this?	What do young children gain from this? Is it offered and is it an option not to join in? **Reflection Point**: Why are we bringing lots of children together when we know they are individuals and like different things? We are teachers of early years, we know the children and we can extend their individual play ideas and group ideas through natural provocation and sustained shared thinking. We do not need to gather children together to do this. Trust your practice and look for moments in play where you are invited in and can extend, then think what next.

The Role of the Educator – Adult-Child Interaction and Routines

How do you view your routine? What do you think about it?

Very importantly, what do the children feel about it, what does their non-verbal and verbal communication tell you?

Giving your time and allowing time is crucial for adult-child interactions. When a child has something to tell you (however they choose to show you) our role in educating is to listen, understand, expand, and extend at the right times throughout the child's time with you. If you are kind and let the children know that their communications matter to you, then you have the key to being an amazing teacher.

Within the routines you have set and discussed with the children, the rules and boundaries should always be fair and up for discussion. The main element is time and allowing flexibility for deep engagement in play, undisturbed amounts of exploring, and creating with varied resources. This is why outside is so great for deep engagement as we discover natural objects and nature, such as molehills. What will the children do when they see a molehill? Perhaps they will decide who might live in them and what they might be. When you have the time they might stamp on it, dig it, squash it, and this is where you as their teacher comment and add some intrigue. This is all play, all learning, and all building brains and expanding cultural capital.

Listen to children – they will show and tell you what they know and how they feel and you can build upon this. Enabling the children to take the lead takes confidence from the adults working with children. Talking with your team and reflecting on this helps smooth the path. As we develop an understanding of how we are teaching children, how they learn, and what they are interested in, this confidence will grow. No one gets everything in life right all the time and we learn from change and understanding what we might do differently. This is a valuable lesson for children – to know that adults are not afraid to try and relish getting it wrong and trying again.

It is important to explain to children that you do not have all the answers. However, you can help them find out by looking in books or on the computer or by asking other people. Embrace being you and be genuine, the children will be more relaxed and you will have created good connections. Adult and child interactions can be strengthened when you talk with children the way you would talk with your friends (obviously keeping on child-level topics). Be genuinely pleased to see them, tell them that you have been waiting for them, and you wondered if they would like to carry on with the game from yesterday. Chat with them and comment, know when to be quiet and give them space and be comfortable with silence. A huge majority of our routine is about doing 'jobs' or 'tasks' rather than observing. Observations are how we get to know children and extend their development.

Ensure in your work, your practice, and especially within your routine that you have time to evaluate daily and be honest. This can be a five-minute chat or discussion with the other adults or by yourself, it can be written down if you want to. You could think about the following points for evaluation as a guide. However, you will know what questions to ask from what sort of day you have had.

Evaluation points you might want to cover (really this depends on the day you have all had):

- What will we do differently tomorrow?
- What was an amazing teaching and learning moment today?
- Were all the children engaged in play?
- Was there a child who just wasn't their usual self today?
- What could we do to extend the play we saw today?
- Do we need to bring resources in for tomorrow?
- What did it feel like for the adults in session today?
- What sort of atmosphere was there?
- What awe and wonder did we see today?
- Were the children asking to do something that didn't fit in with the routine?
- Were there any behaviours that we need to understand more about?
- What did the session feel like for the children? How do you know?

All behaviours are communicating a need; this could be positive or negative, this includes all the adults, children, and families you work with. When we have time within our routine to understand, listen, and name emotions, everyone's well-being and practice become valued. There can be unresolved issues – something that needs talking about yet nobody initiates the conversation. By talking in a daily short evaluation, it avoids escalation and misunderstanding. You can always plan for more talking time if it is needed; however, ten minutes a day is a great place to start. This also feeds into regular statutory supervision. Just a quick note here – one-to-one supervisions are vital in early years practice; they are a time to talk together honestly and openly in order to progress.

Tweaking routines and looking at what really works and what doesn't takes honesty and courage – have a think about the following points as this should really help.

Reflection Point

This is great for team meetings and developing reflective communications.

- What are the routines in your setting?
- Do you have to stick with these routines, if so, why?
- How do you as an individual feel about a flexible routine?
- What are the benefits of having a flexible routine?
- Are there any negatives to having a flexible routine?
- Where is the child in the routine, is their opinion valued?
- How well do adults communicate the routine to children?

> ❖ How many years have you had the same routines?
> ❖ Is it difficult to implement new ideas and change?
> ❖ Do all adults understand the benefits of reviewing routines?

Just a few reminders of what a flexible routine is and is not...

It is not a free-for-all, there are fair boundaries and routines that help create calm and understanding. Children are not rushed and time is viewed as a key element in practice. Deep engagement in play features highly in a flexible routine. Free-flow within the playroom is vital and where possible inside and outside is offered so children have a choice of environments. Children are enabled to choose resources and express their ideas. Tidying up is timely, when a child naturally finishes in one area, they help to keep it looking fabulous for others. Adults model and embrace this, 'wow this is looking beautiful for the other children to play with.' Tidying up does not become negative and a battle of wills, children are given responsibility for small tasks. Resources are respected and cared for and everything has a home. The children begin to know where things belong from a very young age and with encouragement care for their environments both inside and outside. When toys and equipment need cleaning the children help, this is just part of natural play and life. Flexible routines enable trust and understanding about real life and enable children to thrive.

Families and Routines

Think about communicating with families about their routines – dropping off and picking up. What is the child's story, some children have a strict bedtime, others sleep in their parent's bed – each story will be unique.

Understanding a family's routine, home life, and the journey of the child when they are not with us really helps communications. If possible, a home visit before a child starts with an early years provider is helpful and is a great way to gain early understanding and develop a relationship with the child and family.

You may be aware that in the everyday of a child's life you actually spend very little time with them – their main educators from pre-birth are their families and close people around them. To know what life is like for the child we will need to create excellent and meaningful communications with them and their family. This includes the people who drop them off and pick them up.

> ## Reflection Point
>
> - ❖ What are the child's routines at home?
> - ❖ What are people in the child's life called?
> - ❖ Is there a space to celebrate families and bring their photographs into the setting so the child can see them and be reassured? A family photo wall at the children's level in the home corner is a good way to implement this.
>
> A quick case study:
>
> A child is excited as their grandparent is picking him up. The early years practitioner answers the door and says, 'look Gabriele your Grannie is here.' The little boy looks confused and a bit worried. The adult shows him his Grannie through the window, and he says that's not Grannie. The practitioner is a bit worried and is not sure this is right. She goes back out and asks the lady for her password to collect the child. The child is now a little distressed and has picked up that something isn't right. The adult decides to ring Dad just to double-check and describes the lady who has come to pick up. That's right, says Dad, that is Gabriele's 'Nonna.' The little boy is taken to his Nonna (Italian for Grandma) and they cuddle, he looks at his Nonna, and says, 'she say Grannie, you not Grannie.' For the little boy this was a word he didn't know, and he certainly didn't have anyone in his family called Grannie.
>
> Can you see the subtleness and understanding that is needed for every family? The way we comment and ask questions of children and how we listen to their answers non-verbally and verbally is key. Really knowing who they really are and who is in their world matters. We know and totally understand what it is like in everyday practice, and we all get names wrong and call people different things; have this information to hand until we really get to know the child. Young children have all sorts of names for people, and these can vary widely. Thinking of easy ways to become familiar, such as using photos in the home corner with names the child uses for their family, could have made such a difference when we consider the case study.

Reflection Point

What else could you do to develop communication relationships with each individual child you work with?

The all about me resource (see Chapter 7) is extremely useful, this is up-to-date information about the child's likes and dislikes, family, and patterns of play. The child's birth story is important and who they live with – do they have two or more homes and share their time between family? Many children have parents living separately and/or sleep over at the houses of other family members, already you have multiple homes that the child is an important member of.

What hobbies does the family have, what trips do they take, and what are the child's favourite things to do and see? It is very easy to find out which favourite book or programme the child likes and have a poster or toy of this for when they start.

Think about what you know about the child and bring this into their natural play. An example of this could be at the playdough table; playing alongside the child and creating a slide as you know this is the child's favourite piece of equipment at the park. You might make a tiny baby out of playdough as you remember one of the little ones has just had a new sibling. These are simple and subtle ways of communicating – you can comment on what you have created and wait for any responses. The children will be engaged in creating whatever they have decided to, they may choose to comment, and they may not; however, they know you are interested in their lives and that they matter.

A great way to talk about family is to comment on what your family has done; this can often be related to a child's experience. An example of this might be a trip to the hairdresser for one of the children at the setting, they come in with their hair shorter and you comment, they may talk about their experience and this could lead to re-creating this and the child deciding what you will all need. You could mention that you took your child to see the hairdressers where your brother works. The connections you make show again that you understand children have a life outside the setting and you are teaching them about experiences and widening their understanding. Teach and build education from where children's foundations are, understanding what they know, and their experiences and interests are the best place to start.

Communication
Vocabulary Boost – Routines

How can we use routines (however they look in our settings) as an opportunity to boost vocabulary?

The answer is actually quite simple – we talk to the children! Think about the opportunities for children to learn 'new words' as we carry out daily activities that we may not automatically consider to be teaching opportunities.

> **Reflection Point**
>
> Take a moment to consider what happens when we tidy up after snack time. What happens? Who collects the plates and cups? Where does any rubbish go and who gets rid of this? Does the table get wiped and any chairs/tables moved?
>
> It would be very easy in a busy environment for the adults to carry out the above quickly and efficiently so that they can return to playing and interacting with the children but wait – we can use this *routine* situation to teach. Think about the age of the children we are referring to here – 18–24 months, they do not need a running commentary but they really will benefit from hearing what you are doing using a combination of single words and short, simple phrases. The key point here is that we are not missing an opportunity for communication, we can include the children in the routine if they are interested and enjoy the time together.

Speech Sound Boost

The key thing about 'routines,' whether they are flexible or not, is that they typically happen every day, so this gives the adult the opportunity to repeat keywords every day, which in turn enables the child to listen to the keywords regularly. When adults reduce their language and use keywords and short phrases with children in this age group, the child can hear the speech sounds that are being combined to form the word over and over again. We know that repetition is so important for teaching vocabulary so it then follows that when a child hears a word regularly, they are exposed to the sounds of that word and an opportunity to produce this word themselves.

We discussed the benefits of music for speech sound development earlier in the chapter – is there opportunity to add songs to familiar routines?

Speech, Language, and Communication Needs

When/how would we know if a child was struggling with their communication?

Children at this age are beginning to express themselves verbally. By making the communication connection they are developing an understanding that they can influence their environment through their vocalisations and words. For some children though, this can be tricky.

Look

- ❖ Can the child follow simple instructions – 'where's your nose?' 'where's your shoe?'
- ❖ Is the child showing awareness of adults and other children?
- ❖ How does the child play? Do they explore toys and play in a way that you would expect?
- ❖ Does the child respond to their name?

Listen

- ❖ Does the child use any words? We would expect children to typically use between 30 and 50 words by the age of two.

Learn

Take time to observe the child and how they are communicating. Children will be using a lot of non-verbal communication at this stage and it is important that we recognise this and respond. It is important to know if the child has made the 'communication connection' and has the intent to communicate.

Speech and language development in this age range varies immensely between children and so many new skills are being learned. By really understanding how the child is communicating we can begin to explore the nature of any difficulties.

Children need to understand what words mean so that they can then learn to use them to make requests or to share an interaction with another. If a child is struggling to understand words or simple requests, they will need an intervention to develop this.

If a child is not yet using any words to express themselves they may feel frustrated or may become withdrawn, we need to support children to find a way of communicating where their needs can be met – that could be non-verbally through gesture/sign or supporting them to develop words.

At this stage, if you are concerned about a child's communication skills it is essential to discuss these concerns with the child's parents/carers and, if appropriate, support parents to contact their Health Visitor who can explore these concerns in more detail.

HOW CAN WE SUPPORT THE CHILD WITH SPEECH, LANGUAGE, AND COMMUNICATION NEEDS?

Practitioner Toolkit

- ❖ Follow the child's lead
- ❖ Position
- ❖ Interpret-respond

Follow the Child's Lead

Take the time to understand what truly motivates the child. A child needs to be motivated in order to communicate, be that verbally or non-verbally. When we observe what a child chooses to play with and how they choose to play we can follow their lead.

Following a child's lead shows the child that you are interested in them and that you value their ideas. When you follow a child's lead in play you can use the opportunity to **comment** on what they are doing/looking at. This enables you to 'teach' new words and help vocabulary growth.

Position

Where possible, be at the same level as the child – the enables the child to see your mouth when you are talking, they can see how your mouth moves to produce certain speech sounds and is an opportunity for you to role model eye contact.

When you position yourself at the same level as the child it becomes easier to make a connection with the child – you have made yourself more accessible to the child and it will be easier for you to observe how they are communicating.

Interpret-Respond

It is important to respond to any communication attempt that the child makes. When we respond to a child we are showing that child that they matter to us. Children who are struggling to communicate at this stage may point to what they want or may use gestures to communicate. We need to interpret this behaviour and add the language for the child.

The child may be trying to communicate verbally and again, if you are not sure what they are saying look around for clues. What are they looking at, what does their behaviour/body language tell you? **Interpret** the sounds you hear or the gestures you observe and provide the child with the language, for example, the child is looking at a box out of reach and saying, 'bo,' you could hand them the box and comment 'box.'

For target suggestions and interventions, see Chapter 8.

5
TWO TO THREE YEARS

Here we are, the *'terrible twos.'* Let us challenge this misconception that two-year-olds have terrible behaviour and constant tantrums! This can be a wonderful stage of development and often when we really see a child's unique personality developing as they will often share their likes, dislikes, thoughts, and ideas. Up until this age children are often helped to do many everyday things, their clothes are chosen for them, they are bundled in and out of the car without too much resistance, they are fairly happy to play with what they have around them, and they use the cup that you have given them. So, what changes and why do two-year-olds receive such a bad press?

Play and the Environment

Quite simply the answer to a two-year-old being engaged and enabled is 'choice' alongside recognition of the child's thoughts, ideas, and emotions. Let's explore this a little deeper and see how this works in real life, in play, and in the environment.

Whatever environment you are in with a two-year-old they will probably want to explore it, if there is a table, they may want to climb it and if there are toys, they may want to tip them all out, remember this is a time of discovery and immense child development. When we think about environments we relate this to wherever you happen to be. This could be a playroom, however it could also be in a supermarket or at the doctor's surgery, a local café, or a friend's house. The main point to remember is that the adults set the environmental influence with their behaviours, moods, body language, and tone of voice.

Behaviour

How do we relate this to the behaviours of two-year-olds? We know as adults we can be having a great day; this can be a little up and down and everything does not have to go right all the time to have a good day, it is a feeling. We have mostly learned to self-regulate or to ask for support, (co-regulation) when we need it.

You find out some bad news, what do you do? Probably chat with a friend and gain support. Two-year-olds have not learned to do this yet, they cannot self-regulate and they need to have calm people around them to co-regulate them. This doesn't mean everything will run smoothly all the time, it means that when things go a little wrong, which they will, that we contain the child and help them to calm, we lend them a little of ourselves. Without this, a two-year-old will not know how to cope with their emotions and the situation can escalate very quickly. Think of it as an emotional teaching moment, what is the real problem, what is the emotion that the child needs help with? We are pretty sure that if we all saw an adult being very upset then we would help, so why would we not help a child?

Consider the following key reflective question:

How do two-year-olds learn?

Understanding this enables everyone working or living with them to realise that it is a stage of key development that really needs understanding and demystifying. Viewing this age group as dynamic, funny, able, and ready to take on the world is a really positive way to understand them and will also help you unpick what each individual child requires to grow and develop securely.

> **Reflection Point**
>
> Are their emotional and physical experiences supported by people who really care and understand them?
>
> - What are our expectations of this age group?
> - How much choice do two-year-olds have in their daily lives?
> - Why do two-year-olds become so upset so quickly?
> - Why do two-year-olds require so much attention?
> - Are two-year-olds deliberately becoming overwhelmed?
> - How do adults in your early years setting co-regulate a two-year-old?
>
> When we look at young children becoming overwhelmed it is usually because expectations can be too high. We all know what it is like as adults to be tired and hungry, and we can usually stop, eat, and rest (even if only for a little while). Young children can often go beyond this point and when you ask them to do something, at times it becomes too much for them.
>
> Provide regular opportunities for eating and building in time for the children to view relaxation as a positive opportunity throughout their day. Children may just lay on the floor,

play, and chat to themselves – the point to acknowledge here is that it is how the child chooses to relax (this is not a group story or circle time, this is individual to them). One child may like to snuggle and look at a book, another might like to lay on the grass and watch the trees and clouds. It is important for us to recognise when the children need time and space and respect this.

Is there always a time in the day where children become upset or cross? Reflect on your environment and routine – why might this be? How could you offer choice and time, how could you ensure that children have time to understand the next transition and are they emotionally supported to do this?

Choice

When we talk about choice we can also think of a limited choice, as otherwise this can become overwhelming for the child. If you wanted a child to help tidy up, the adult could say, 'would you like to put the book or the dolly away?', 'Would you like to carry your bag or your coat?', 'Would you like to wear your wellies or shoes?'; showing young children the actual object helps them to understand what is required of them.

Teaching works so much better when we focus on what the child requires and the adult values everyday natural moments. In life we require all young children to have the opportunity to be taught and understood and to be given the confidence to choose and to be a dynamic part of their everyday learning. The connection between the young child and their future must be cherished and understood as there is no way to re-live childhoods. In early years the connections we create with every child have a direct impact now and for their future lives.

Communication
What Would We Expect to See/Hear?

By two and a half years:

- May have up to 500 words in their vocabulary
- Understand instructions with two keywords 'get a teddy and a dolly'
- May use two- to three-word sentences 'mummy get book'

By three years:

- ❖ Using up to 700 words… Following instructions containing three keywords such as 'Put teddy under the table'
- ❖ Using sentences of four or more words
- ❖ Grammar is developing – little words such as 'me,' 'a,' 'the,' and adding past tense –'ed' – such as 'walked,' but some over-generalisation, such as 'runned'
- ❖ Begin to talk outside of the here and now
- ❖ Ask lots of questions using 'what,' 'where,' and 'why'

During this age range, communication really takes off! Children progress from using single words to name what they can see to forming sentences and asking questions. Two-year-olds are busy, their brains are growing at an incredible rate and they are beginning to understand the power they can have in the world. We can join them on their journey of speech and language development and really understand their personality and what their interests are.

Vocabulary

Top Tips

Allow space and choice – this is a really important point to explore. As we have mentioned, two-year-olds are developing independence and we need to respect this. We will still have many opportunities for teaching moments but these will be more meaningful if we give the child space to explore the toys and resources and enable them to learn to play in a way that makes sense to them.

When children are interested and deeply engaged, we can add language when the moment is right. Be mindful that we don't need to be talking to children all the time, a well-placed comment shows that we are interested in what they are doing but we are giving them space to develop their own ideas.

Choice is so important for this age range, we know that two-year-olds need to feel autonomous, and offering choice, whether that is food, clothes, or toys, will ensure that the child feels that the 'power' is theirs.

Take turns to speak – listen carefully and give the child time to finish. This is important. Two-year-olds will have their own thoughts and ideas but they may not yet have the skills to communicate these effectively. It is essential that we are 'present' and are actively listening to these children when they communicate with us. It can be easy to anticipate what the child is going to say or what they want but when we do this and do not give the child time to express themselves we disempower them. This is a teaching moment – we need to role model how listening and turn-taking in conversation work and when we don't give the child the opportunity to communicate or finish what they were going to say, we are not being a good communication role model.

Remember – children will learn new words and how to use them by watching you and how you communicate and interact with others.

During this stage, children start to develop their understanding and use of grammar – it is very common to hear 'I runned.' The role of the adult here is to teach by modelling – 'you ran.' We never need to ask children to repeat after us as this stops the natural flow of conversation (and must be really annoying for the child), but it is important that we notice when there is a teaching moment and respond.

Speech Sounds

We would typically expect to understand approximately 50 per cent of what a two-year-old is telling us, so we are still not expecting all speech sounds to be used accurately.

You may hear children missing the ends of words – this is called final consonant deletion, for example, 'hat' is pronounced as 'ha.' This is a typical developmental process and is not something that we would be concerned about at this stage. If we observe this process in a child's speech, we model and say it as they would if they could.

Another process that we may observe in our two-year-olds is fronting. This is where sounds which are produced at the back of the mouth 'k' and 'g' are produced at the front of the mouth, for example '**c**up' is pronounced as '**t**up' and '**g**irl' may be produced as '**d**irl.' Again, this is a typical developmental process and would not be a concern for our two- to three-year-olds.

Stopping is the term used to describe when a long, friction sound, such as 's' or 'f,' is produced as short, explosive sounds 'd' or 'b', for example, '**s**un' is produced as '**d**un' and '**f**ish' may be produced as '**b**ish.'

These processes occur as the child is learning how to coordinate their muscles to produce a vast range of speech sounds and our role is to teach by modelling. When you hear a child speaking using the above processes, repeat back what they have said, modelling the accurate use of speech sounds but try not to interrupt the flow of conversation, this is not as easy as it sounds.

The Role of the Educator – Adult-Child Interaction

Let's take a moment to reflect and think about quality interactions in practice with two-year-olds.

The quality of interactions and connections that adults create with young children is completely crucial to their current and future well-being, communication, and brain development. A huge responsibility, yes, it is an enormous responsibility! A career path into the early years arena should always be taken with respect for this role, with understanding and research into what working with young children entails. Being supported by amazing professionals and learning how to interact with and value children is a great starting point. There are many courses, debates, books, and network groups to further education and understanding of this role.

Two-year-olds are one of the most intriguing age groups adults can work with. You can certainly create fantastic, funny, respectful, and engaging connections and interactions by really getting to know the children and observing what interests them. Acknowledge their emotions.

You may have worked with people who find it totally natural to be at the child's level, listen and extend play. The key with two-year-olds is to be an amazing listener however the child chooses to communicate. This is where understanding natural behaviours comes into play; spotting where a child may become distressed or overexcited, where they have asked for attention several times.

They could be asking for attention from you by pulling on your skirt, jumping up and down, moving your face; think to yourself – this child has something to tell or show me. Now sometimes these actions by two-year-olds become misinterpreted as being 'rude,' seeking attention. It is not! It is the child's way of communicating because usually if an adult has missed a cue in the past, then you can be sure by doing one of these actions or by shouting or screaming the child will have gained some adult attention.

So here is your choice – are you going to say, 'don't do that, it's rude' or are you going to say, 'I hear you'? Adults can say 'I hear you' physically with their connections and body language. If you are talking or playing with another child, try to include the child who requires your connection as well. If you really cannot do this, say to the child, 'I hear you, let's get someone to help you.' It is alright to not meet every need of the child, however you must acknowledge them and enable them to be seen.

Young children seek you out to feel loved, safe, and secure, to know that they matter and are important. If when they seek this, it is batted away or they receive negative responses their actions may become louder, they might hit out, and they may be frustrated or perhaps they will withdraw. Either way, they will gain negative attention and their confidence will not be enabled positively.

Think about how you respond, is it a reaction or a considered response? Reactions are for when someone is immediately going to hurt themselves – for example you see a pair of scissors falling off the shelf and you react by catching them. We respond to children; we work with our thinking brain and fine-tune our professional responses. Adults should be very aware of how they appear to young children, what is the expression on an adult's face when they are responding to a child, how close are they to them, what are the adult's hands doing? What tone of voice do you use?

Child's action two-year-olds	*Adults' response two-year-olds*
A child comes over to join in with the train play, there is no space, and they start to become cross.	• Notice the child, name the emotion, 'Aggie you seem cross.' • Ask 'would you like to play with us?' • 'Shall we make room, we could start another train set?' To avoid this scenario notice when children want to join in and say, 'I see you'; this can be with a smile and positive body language, 'let's make some space for…'
A child is tugging at you and wants you; you are in the middle of changing another child.	• Acknowledge the child, use positive body language. • Say 'I am changing…you could ask Sally to help you.' Where possible ask another team member to help with the child. It is alright for you to say that you will be with them very soon. Noticing the child is key, you cannot always attend to every need.
A child is sad as her parent has just left; you are talking to another parent.	• Notice the child. • Name the emotion. • Respond physically with an offer of a cuddle, pick him up, or just sit with him – this is where knowing each child really helps. The child must come first at this point. If you really need to talk to the parent, ask them to wait and settle the child with another team member. If you work alone then tell the parent that you will speak with them later once everyone is settled.
A child keeps getting upset every time the doorbell rings.	• Acknowledge the child's emotion and tell them they are safe. • Work out why this is and what is worrying the child. • Show them the doorbell and how it works. • Ask them to help you answer the door. • Ensure they are with an adult when you know it is home time. What does the doorbell mean to them – is it when parents pick up? Are they anxious because they think their parent is picking up and then it is another parent?
A child asks for a cuddle; you are just about to read a story.	• Cuddles come first, work the story into natural play and experiences. • Really observe the children at storytime, are they engrossed? What is their body language telling you? • Enable children to leave the story circle when they have heard all they want to. If you decide to have a whole group storytime with two-year-olds this will need to be really intriguing – use props and voices, follow the child's cues, and do not ever worry about getting to the end of the story. We want children to love reading and this is where it starts. Reading one-to-one or with small groups of children who want to snuggle up and have a story is far more beneficial.

You are helping the children to put their coats on and a child is taking a long time to get ready.	<ul><li>Remember to build teaching how to put coats and clothes on into your flexible routine.</li><li>If a child is happy to take their time and keeps on trying, adults support this.</li><li>If a child asks for help, then use this as a way to teach them. Let them know that you learned this when you were little. Make a game of it and never underestimate these golden moments of teaching and enabling children to learn life skills.</li><li>If you all have to go out the door together quickly then take coats with you and help the child once you are outside.</li><li>With two-year-olds it is best to take smaller groups out who are ready first and then the other children can follow with another adult at their pace.</li></ul>
A child throws a soft toy across the room.	<ul><li>We pick it up and say we can throw it outside, let's see what we can find and take it out.</li></ul>
A child throws a hard toy across the room.	<ul><li>We pick it up and say we can throw it outside, this is hard it will hurt someone. Let's see what we can find and take it outside to throw.</li><li>In both scenarios if you cannot go straight out, find soft objects and a space where children can throw inside. Let the children help to create this.</li></ul>
A child is desperate to go outside, they are standing by the closed door and starting to get frustrated.	<ul><li>Offer free-flow, this means inside and outside at the same time; this is hugely beneficial for young children and enables them to have deeper engagement in the environment they learn best in.</li><li>The children have a choice and deeper engagement in play, which then creates opportunities for positive child and brain development. Understanding and implementing child development practice means we give the child the best possible start to their life. The children have communicated their needs and you have responded as an active listener.</li></ul>

By understanding these young children's attachments and what they are telling you, you can create and strengthen the child's confidence and relationship patterns.

Dropping Off/Settling Children 'Attachment Led'

Dropping off and settling children is arguably one of the most important times in a two-year-old's day, and it is certainly one of the key skills adults who work in early years are required to understand.

Let's explore this a little deeper – what is happening for the child before they are even dropped off to you? What emotions could they be feeling on the way to your setting? The most important people in their lives, their family, trust you to look after, educate, and treasure their child, in this case a child who has been on the planet and in their lives only for 24 months. Those 24 months have already been a whirlwind of emotions and change. Families have chosen you to help grow their child and you really are a wider part of their extended family. You are one of the child's first understanding of the wider world around them.

Children are programmed to be wary of strangers and when the child firsts meets you this is what you are to them. Settling children in and building a relationship with their family really helps the foundations of 'drop off times.' The longer you can settle a child and not rush their attachment with you the better. Some children will settle very quickly, and others won't. Neither is right nor wrong; the children are individuals.

When you look at your settling in procedures, is the unique child taken account of? What has the family already told you about the child and what is the child's communication telling you?

If families do not come into your setting, what other ways can you help the children to settle and know that they are safe? Ideas you could use are your outside play areas, picnics, games, home visits. Outside is often a calmer environment with natural sounds and less pressure on children.

If families do come into your setting, can they do this at their child's pace and for short periods of time? Is there a space where they could sit and relax and still be in the room with their child?

The child can check in with their parent whilst getting to know you. You can also start to create trusting relationships with the family and the child. The more time you can give to developing attachments the easier it will be for the child when they are left with you and their family is not present.

Ensure that you have child-led interest toys available, also ensure that key adults are available to help settle the child. With a two-year-old who does not want to be left, then take it very slowly, allow plenty of time before the parent really does have to go. If the child is upset, asking another family member to support their settling with you works well.

- ❖ Have the child's natural comforting objects with them and ready to use at your setting should they need them. If they need their blanket and their comforter to start with then that is how they are telling you they feel safe.
- ❖ If a child brings in a transitional object from home let them keep it with them.
- ❖ Only settle for short periods of time without the parent.
- ❖ Ensure that the parent/family are first to pick the child up until the child has really settled and knows you well.
- ❖ If a child is playing and settled, ensure you check in with them with a smile or a thumbs up.
- ❖ If transitions are hard and unsettling to start with then really think – are they totally necessary for now?
- ❖ Changing times – many two-year-olds wear nappies; ask the parent to change the child during a few of the settling sessions, to show the child where they get changed.

Respect

Very importantly, if a two-year-old communicates to you that you cannot change them, then this will need to be respected. They are not yet ready for this level of trust and intimacy with you.

We totally understand that this may be unusual in practice, however it is very important that children have ownership of their own bodies, and we cannot disrespect this. In practice, we make this very clear to parents and families before they start. We ask them to bring the child in a clean nappy or change them at drop off. We will change the child the first time with their parent or family member present. The child needs to trust that their communications are listened to and cannot be just brushed aside because it doesn't fit our routine. It may be that we ask for a member of the family who is able to come to the setting and change the child if the child does not want us to change them.

This does not happen often as we take the time to build robust attachments with the child; however, it does happen and parents are willing to come back and change the child as they know that the child's communication is valued and understood. The alternative of a child crying and being upset as someone they do not really know changes their nappy is not a great start in life. As kind and comforting as we are in early years this is an area for consideration, discussion, and thought.

Children settle fairly quickly when they are listened to and understood and in an environment and atmosphere of care and professional love. No child should be left crying at the door, it is a horrible way for the parent to leave and the child to start their new adventures. Time for settling and the reasons for this are key to robust future transitions for children.

The Physical Environment and Attachment-Led Practice

Creating attachment-led practice is crucial when working with all children. To understand this, we need to explore our own childhoods and motivations. Great practice and teaching starts with knowing who we are and what our early years ethos is.

Here are some reflective questions exploring motivation for working with young children, developing research and practice.

What do you feel is your role in early years and why do you work with two-year-olds? Sometimes the answers are as simple as, I stumbled into early years as I have my own children, or I have always liked children.

Do you take your role seriously and understand the responsibility you have in enabling futures? Do you feel this is a professional route for you and your career? What are your goals and how will you be an advocate for early years and the children you work with?

Which of your childhood influences do you feel you bring into everyday practice?

Do your thoughts about how a child should be reared and nurtured relate to current research in early years education?

The Power Balance

As we know adults create the child's physical environment from just being there. The adult has the power. If you tell the children, they cannot go outside because it is raining then this is what they will have to do. As an adult if we told you that you cannot go out because it is raining, and you really needed to go out, what would you do or say?

What is the thought and research behind two-year-olds not accessing their outside in all weathers? Where are the teachable moments that say it is wrong to go outside and explore? Now, we believe that everyone comes into early years with a good heart and a love for children, they want to do the right thing for the child. This is fantastic, however every adult's practice must be supported by research and understanding of how children learn and what deep engagement in play really looks like in the everyday environment.

If there was a formula for physical environments for two-year-olds it could look something like:

1. **Dynamic** person.
2. **Inspiring** adult, observing, and extending.
3. **Love**, kindness, and understanding.
4. **Time** to play, think, relax, and for the child to be themselves
5. Child in an **engaged physical environment** – great for child development!

All of which equals an environment where the child is listened to and can engage and where their learning is extended through their interests.

DILT = EPE. Here it is as an acronym. It does seem a bit flashy, but we know everyone remembers things differently, so if this helps then please do use it. The diagram says it all really, children need a fantastic person who inspires, loves, and teaches them at the child's own pace and through the child's interests. The adult adds to these interests and extends learning at the right time and at the right pace.

Attachment-Led Practice

Attachment-led practice requires you to notice, care, and act. Let's look at the going outside in the rain scenario again; in attachment-led practice with two-year-olds we now know we really need to notice their non-verbal communication. With a child standing by the window and looking at the rain, what could you do next? Where could you take the next 'in the moment' educational step? Where could it lead?

It is raining scenario:

1. You could say, 'let's come away from the window and play with the playdough.'
2. You could talk about the drops of rain and describe them.
3. You could think, I wonder if this child has really felt what it is like to be in the rain.
4. You could open the window and feel and smell the rain.
5. You could ask, 'shall we go and explore in the rain?'
6. You could open the door and have a look together.
7. You could go out with umbrellas and wellingtons.
8. You could go without umbrellas.
9. You could stamp, jump, sit in puddles.
10. You could open your mouths and taste the rain, you could see where it is coming from, you could stamp and jump and sit in puddles and you could have fun with the children.

Once you have explored the rain you could think, 'where shall we go with this next?'

How will we explore this idea naturally in the everyday? Perhaps you might put some sponges in with the water play and see what happens; you might comment on how the water is being sucked up, using new words such as 'absorbed' and showing what this means as the children play. You might relate this to the clouds and where rain comes from when you are next outside and looking at the clouds.

Children can learn so much from nature and an interactive, inspiring adult. What we don't really need to do is all create the same cloud picture, or all sit down together and talk about it. Two-year-olds are far too young for this and it will just stifle their creativity.

Have creative things at hand that the children can explore and comment on what they do. The difference here is that they are choosing to be creative and not being told how to create, they are exploring and experimenting. Depending upon their ideas and patterns of play their creation will look very different from every other child's and this is a good thing.

As educators we have a choice, shall we create a cloud with all the children from cotton wool or shall we go out and look at clouds, noticing how they move and what they really look like? Our natural environment can teach so much more than we could teach from a rote activity. As adults in early years, we comment and extend to help young children learn and develop.

Two-year-olds are dynamic, active, and physical learners. They need to move, roll, rock, run, swing, dive, collapse in a heap, and then swing themselves or their arms around some more. They are making sense of the world and where they are in it, they are making sense of their own physical sense of self. It really is not natural for them to be inside and sitting at tables.

Floor level is great for this age group, so if you have a painting area, try to make this on the floor; you could cover a palette with paper, the children can continue to build on their ideas daily. Instead of taking everything home or clearing all the paintings away at the end of the day, you could let the children see what their paintings look like at the next sessions, and they could keep adding to them.

Having paint and various media to add on session after session really helps to explore creativity. A big canvas on the floor and doing the same with this is a great way to enhance your environment, as when the children and adults think it is finished and come to a natural end (this could be months) then you have your own work of art to put on the wall, you can add everyone's name who has taken part in this wonderful creation and even have a timescale of photos of what the painting and creating process looked like.

Relationships and Conflict

When you create the physical environment, you will really need to understand what and who two-year-olds need to enhance their development. You and the children are in this together – yes, you are an adult and at times you will need to put fair boundaries in place and help to solve squabbles and disagreements, and when you do this think about what the children are learning and help them to develop empathy and build emotional intelligence. This will happen only if the adult is the positive role model for this and the children observe this kindness throughout their environment.

Here is an aspect that may be a little tricky though it must be addressed; at times you and your colleagues will need to speak to team members and/or managers who fail to understand the influence of their physical presence and the tone of voice upon children. Does the physical and emotional atmosphere in the room change when they walk in? Why might this be? What would help to change this?

When you are creating an amazing physical environment, you are ensuring that everyone in this space speaks kindly and with respect to children. The children relax and trust the adults and their safe space and then and only then can they learn.

The Role of the Educator – Adult-Child Interaction and Attachment-Led Practice

The role of the educator with two-year-olds is to be their ally and to ensure that each child is heard, and their childhood valued. This stage is a critical stage in development and the adults who make up the social family of two-year-olds are the main influences in teaching the children about life. The child learns from their immediate and wider community, and you play a key role in this. They will start to make friendships between the ages of two and three, they may play alongside others at the beginning; however, nearing three they often decide who makes them laugh and who they like being around.

Children learn when they are secure and feel safe. The connections that you make with the children you work with and with their families are very important. Adults in a two-year-old's life will need to be consistent; you must have patience and be understanding. The role you take is a professional one, with research (such as reading this book), and continual lifelong learning into the field of early years being a crucial part of this career. We cannot have 'off days' with the children; we are professionals. However, we know that as professionals and humans we all have ups and downs in our lives, so how does this fit into the everyday demands of early years practice?

> ### Reflection Point
> ❖ What does practising as a professional in early years mean to you?
> ❖ How do you look after your own mental well-being?
> ❖ If you know that you are not well enough mentally or physically to practise, what do you do?

> ❖ If you know you need some support to practise for whatever reason, what do you do?
> ❖ What support is there for adults who are not coping and who need help?
> ❖ Do your emotions affect the connections you make with the young children you work with?

Emotional Regulation

We lead by example with children, and this means we show them that sometimes everything does not go how they thought it might and you lend the child some of your own emotional regulation to help them learn. Now, you can only do this if you can regulate your emotions and if you have the emotional intelligence to know when you require time for yourself and when you need help.

Having an 'off day,' where it's all a bit up in the air, is alright at home if this is balanced with calm, fun, and other exciting times. Children learn that there are blips and that you can recover from these. No child is born with emotional regulation and resilience; it takes a long time to learn and understand emotions. Many adults are still learning, and we go on to learn as we experience different emotions in our lives. There may be one day where you are fine and nothing really bothers you, then the next day you have the same routine, however everything goes a little wrong. Perhaps you miss the bus or forget your lunch and someone is a bit rude to you; how you react may differ, however you use your emotional regulation and intelligence to calm yourself. Now if something bigger came along like a loved one being poorly or your child being upset going to school every day this may start to have a knock-on effect and you will need to ensure that you build more time in for you.

As a professional do you feel that if you or one of your team is upset, angry, sad, overexcited, depressed, or anxious, that this will not transcend into everyday practice? It is perfectly acceptable to have feelings and emotions – we need these to work with children; however, we are professionals, and we must take our role very seriously. There are times in your early years career where you will need to take a break and reflect on how you feel; life changes and circumstances will change throughout life. We just need to remember that to teach we must be well ourselves. Taking time for you is key to creating connections with children and avoid burning out. You can give only what you have, and you must have reserves for you.

Regular evaluations, quick morning chats, and regular supervision are paramount to enable robust teaching and emotional regulation for you, your team, and the families you work with.

Once the children arrive at the setting everyone needs to be in the moment and focused on the families and children and create an environment of well-being and connections where children thrive. This does not mean we are all dancing and singing all the time – it means we are in a space where we can recognise young children's emotional needs and we can connect with them and co-regulate them so that they can thrive and learn.

The Words We Use

Communication creates connections. Quality interactions and robust attachments are built on trust and security; let's think about things we might say, our families might have said to us, or what you hear others say in daily practice.

Your own childhood, how were you spoken to as a child, how did it make you feel?

Ways of talking to children – it is always better if you can talk and communicate with children rather than at and to them. Here are a few things that you may have heard in your life or in education:

You are doing my head in.
I have told you and won't tell you again.
Why are you not listening to me?
I will use my teacher voice.
I will have to tell your Mummy, Daddy, Grannie.
You can see that I am busy.
Because I said so.
No, I can't help you put your coat on (in response to a child getting really frustrated).
No, leave him he can do it.
No, we are not going out you can see it is raining.
Why do the children keep bothering me?

Reflect on how children may feel when spoken to like this. How would you feel if you were spoken to like this? Remember as adults we are often empowered to question and put in our own boundaries, which are listened to because we are big.

Positioning

Body positioning – how are the adults positioned around the young children? Are they using their body language to create a physical environment where we would all like to be? Adults should be aware of how much space they take up, what their facial expressions are and what it feels like to be around them. Never get too close to a child especially if you feel you are cross. Never whisper in their ear if you are telling them off, this is scary and does not build trust. Be at the child's level but not right in their face or space; children require autonomy and space to thrive. Sit, eat with children, and enjoy their company. Think of creating a safe communication space for everyone who steps through your door.

Children notice all communication especially when it is not supportive. Shaming, threatening, damaging self-esteem is not early years practice, it is detrimental to children and their confidence. If you hear or observe these types of practice professionally challenge. You are an advocate for the child, ask for support with this if you need help. We have futures in our hands and the words we utter can damage the children. Reflect, discuss, and change outdated practice.

Cuddles, hugs, and physical closeness – these are great ways for many children to know that they are understood and important in your life, and they create attachments that are healthy. Some children don't like a hug and that is alright too, a touch on their arm may be enough to reassure them. Some children do not like to be close to others at all. Working with individual children we soon start to understand what helps them to feel loved and secure and what doesn't. A note here: if a child communicates to you that they want a hug or to be picked up it is important that we respond kindly; we care, we love, and we educate. Our early years role is to unpick each child's needs and communications and interpret these to enable the child to develop and thrive.

Families and Attachment-Led Practice

Early years can really help to ensure that families understand their crucial role in their child's life. They are the child's first teacher; the child learns about life, communications, and connections from them. Families know so much about the child and we can learn much from them. We understand the unique child and the need for individuality, and families are no different – each one has varying dynamics and is created differently.

We might think we know about family relationships, and we might even judge; however, we never know what it is really like to be a member of another family. We do not really know what life is like for the child in their home.

As early years professionals, we can look at our own practice and demonstrate to families what this will look like for their child when they are in the early years setting. When communicating with families, honesty is always best right from the start. Ask them to come into a session and see what really happens in the everyday, it then gives the parent the chance to ask questions and gives you the opportunity to demonstrate your quality interactions in a natural way. It also demonstrates that you are not a show setting, you are real people, and the children are also.

Reflection Point

What could your response be?

- ❖ A parent comes along for a visit, you are outside and stamping in puddles and digging in the mud and they say that they don't really want their child to get wet when they start with you.
- ❖ You offer water and milk; however, a parent wants their child to have juice.
- ❖ A parent wants to drop off and go straight away; however, their child is very upset and unsettled.

There are probably many more thoughts around this that you may have come across in practice. The main thought here is the research behind your practice and the adults who work in the setting knowing why you practise in a certain way, understanding your ethos and embedding this in your practice and ensuring that families are included and understand your practice well.

Parents who really do not want their child to get wet or muddy have genuine reasons, it makes total sense to them. The reasons could be that they cannot afford to keep buying new clothes or washing clothes. It could be that they were not allowed to have messy play when they grew up. It could also be that they may worry their child will get too cold. They may not be aware of the benefits of exploring outside and there could be many reasons we have not covered.

This is the time to evidence your practice with research and share the ethos of your setting. Early years research has reams of articles, blogs, books, and resources showing the benefits of outdoor play. The early years professional role here would be to share this knowledge. Creating relationships of honesty and not promising what we cannot deliver is key. Not every setting is for every family. Clear, kind, and honest communication from the first time you meet builds robust relationships.

For example, offering milk and water would be because you have looked at what children require for a healthy diet now and in the future. Also, concern must be taken as to what is needed to reduce tooth decay in young children. So, there is thought, reasoning, and science as to why juice is not offered. There are many ways that children can reduce daily sugar in their diet, and therefore early years settings have a requirement to teach children about their oral health. You can communicate this to families by asking dental nurses to come into the practice and have a family evening around this.

Inclusive Environment

Everyday communications with families are key to creating an inclusive physical environment where people are trusted and feel valued. Ensure that the children have communities of all colours represented in your setting; children must see themselves and others in their environment to feel a real part of the wider world. Create an audit of your environment –what are you good at including and what is missing? Who is in your local community? Include this, who isn't in your community? Include this too. We can only understand the world if we know who lives in it, then we see everyone as equally important. Ensure that bias is addressed and that all children are valued equally.

Let's take a look at the last reflection point; a child being dropped off and being upset, understanding this is very important for attachment-led practice.

- What do you and the adults around you think is the best thing to do?
- How would you comfort this child?
- Would you ask the parent to stay?
- Do you feel your settling sessions are robust?
- Do the children really know you and the team?
- What is in place to emotionally contain the child and the family?
- Is the child expected to stop crying quickly?
- Do you give the child time and name their emotions?
- Do you stay near and offer hugs?

Distracting can work, however this is a little like papering over the cracks. A child who knows that their emotions are contained and they are co-regulated will play when they are ready. They may spend several sessions on your lap and need lots of reassurance. Ensure that the time that parents leave is very short and build this up slowly.

Remember in the natural world two-year-olds are relying on their loved ones to survive, our primitive brain is saying, 'why am I being left?' and 'am I safe here?' You are showing the child that yes, they are safe and that their main carers always come back. Settling is a great learning process; it is the start of becoming independent and how this is managed and understood by all adults working in early years and all families is fundamental to children's development. By really listening to the child's communication of 'I am scared' you are creating patterns of positive transitions not only now but also for the future.

Discovering what families can offer and what hidden talents they have brings the children's life experience into everyday reality and practice. Do you know what hobbies and careers the families have or have had? Do you know what resources the families could help you create or mend? Every intake of new children and families brings something special into your setting. Give the families and children ownership of their space. You and the children will thrive with more experience around you and a community of practice that really does treasure, welcome, include, and understand each and every family.

Communication
Vocabulary Boost – Attachment-Led Practice

We have discussed the importance of understanding the emotions of two-year-olds and how they learn. It is important to note that these emotions can feel overwhelming for the young child, who may not know why they are feeling the way they are feeling.

We have provided examples of how to 'contain' children by observing their emotions and behaviours and providing a label for it – 'you seem very sad' and by introducing the vocabulary of emotions we are supporting the child to make the link between their thoughts, their emotions, and their behaviours. As children grow and develop, this knowledge will help them to manage the more difficult emotions.

We know that younger children may not have the vocabulary to talk about how they are feeling and so we teach the vocabulary in the moment of the experience. Remember to observe when a child is happy, excited, or relaxed – these are all important emotions to learn about as well as the noticeable sad, angry, or frustrated.

We can also support children to develop empathy and an understanding of the emotions of others, we can observe when another child is deeply engaged in their play or laughing with a friend and we can comment on this: 'look, Amy looks happy.'

Children need to know what is happening in their daily routine and knowing when your parent/carer is leaving you or coming to collect you are two very important parts of the day. Children at this age will not yet understand the concept of time and so be mindful not to use phrases such as 'Mummy's coming in five minutes' or even 'Mummy's coming soon' as this is meaningless to the child. It can be helpful to use visual timetables to support the child's understanding of time and these can be detailed with all the transitions of the day or can be as simple as a 'now and then' board – 'now we are singing and then Mummy comes.'

This early introduction to the concept of time and sequencing will be useful core skills on which to build further mathematical concepts and understanding.

Speech Sound Boost – Attachment-Led Practice

Can we support speech sound development through attachment-led practice?

Well, the simple answer is yes. We know that we are role models for children and as we are supporting children with their emotional development by naming their emotions and offering comfort when needed we are also probably going to position ourselves so that we are accessible to the child. We may join them on the floor, we pick them up for a cuddle if that is what has been requested, but what is likely is that the child will see our face and will then see how our mouth moves to produce words.

But here is the key point – children must feel safe and secure to access their learning environment. So, this brings us to the topic of 'dummies.'

Dummy Use

Speech therapists advise that a child does not have a dummy after the age of one (ideally, not once babbling and talking starts). Many children are still using a dummy after the age of two and we can support parents with this. A dummy can play a very important role in comforting a child, but what do we need to know?

- ❖ Extended dummy use can result in overuse of the muscles at the front of the mouth compared to the muscles at the back of the mouth.
- ❖ Stomach and mouth infections – due to bacteria on the dummy.
- ❖ Dental problems such as open bite and crossbite – this can then result in a 'lisp' type quality to the speech.
- ❖ Reduced babbling and experimentation with sounds – it is very difficult to talk with a dummy in your mouth. Imagine having a dummy in your mouth and trying to say 'baby' and 'teddy' – it is impossible to say the 'b,' 't,' and 'd' sounds accurately as there is an object preventing the articulators coming together.
- ❖ Overuse of a dummy will often result in a 'backing' pattern to speech, where sounds which should be produced at the front of the mouth are produced at the back of the mouth – 't' is produced as a 'k,' 'toe' would be produced as 'koe.' This is due to the dummy preventing the tongue lifting up at the front of the mouth to touch just behind the top teeth and so the tongue lifts at the back of the mouth, where it is free to make contact with the roof of the mouth.

    How and when a parent chooses to remove the dummy is a personal decision, but we can provide information as to why we need to monitor dummy use in two-year-olds. Our role here is not to preach and certainly not to judge families, but we do have a role to educate about the impact of dummy use on speech.

If a child needs the dummy in order to settle into the environment then this must be the priority. We can compromise here and support the child to remove the dummy once they feel comfortable and support them to take it out of their mouth when they are talking.

Speech, Language, and Communication Needs

When/how would we know if a child was struggling with their communication?

Look

- Can the child focus their attention on a self-chosen activity for around two or three minutes?
- Does the child point or show you what they want instead of using words? We would expect the child to be using words at this stage.
- How does the child behave around peers? Do they move away or become distressed if another child approaches them?
- Can the child follow instructions containing two keywords? 'Put the apple in the cup' when there is a choice to be made between 'apple' and an alternative and 'cup' and an alternative.

Listen

- Is the child using only single words to communicate? We would expect a child to have enough single words in their vocabulary to be able to start forming short phrases and then sentences.
- Are you struggling to understand most of what the child is saying?
- How is the child using the words they have? Do they ask for things they want or just comment on what they can see?

Learn

We are not expecting children aged two to three years to have clear speech. They are still developing their speech sounds and learning how to combine them into words. As a rough guide, you can expect to understand approximately 50 per cent of what a two-year-old is saying.

What we do want to see is children at this stage using their communication skills for a range of reasons – to comment on what they can see, to make requests, to refuse, to ask questions, and for developing relationships with others.

Two to Three Years

As you observe the children in your setting, notice the children who are not yet using any words – how do they get their needs met? If they want something, how do they let you know? What do they do to keep themselves busy?

It is also important that at this stage we notice what a child **is** doing rather than focusing on what they can't yet do. If a child is using some natural gesture to communicate, consider using some simple signs to enable the child to have a means of communicating with others. See Chapter 8 for more information on using 'sign' with children.

As with all stages, if you are concerned about a child's communication skills and it is impacting their ability to engage in the setting then ask for advice and support. Most speech and language therapy departments have websites with details on how to refer a child and other advice and suggested activities.

HOW CAN WE SUPPORT THE CHILD WITH SPEECH, LANGUAGE, AND COMMUNICATION NEEDS?

Practitioner Toolkit

- ❖ Offer choice
- ❖ Find the motivation
- ❖ Respond-repeat-extend
- ❖ Offer strategies

Offer Choice

Offering a choice between two items is a really useful way to support children to learn and use words. When we say, 'offer a choice,' be careful; we are not saying to a child 'would you like milk?' Yes, this is a choice but the child is not given the opportunity to hear and use the target vocabulary and instead they are given the option to say 'yes' or 'no.' By offering 'would you like milk or water?' we are providing a vocabulary teaching moment as we label each item as we show it to the child and we also give the child the opportunity to hear how we have said the word, providing a clear speech role model.

Children who are non-verbal may indicate their choice through eye pointing, reaching, or pointing, and it is important that we accept this means of communication. We want the child to know that we have understood their communication and they receive their preferred choice. Our role here is to add the word to match the non-verbal communication, for example, child reaches for milk, adult models 'milk.'

Note of caution – manners are important and we can role model please and thank you to children but if we are supporting a child who is non-verbal, the priority is to model specific vocabulary as this will be more useful to them rather than please or thank you.

If we offer this choice on a daily basis we can gradually extend the pause time after we have offered the choice, giving the child more opportunity to verbalise their preference. It is very important that we are not putting any pressure on a child to respond. We are not 'waiting' until they say the word before they get their preference, we are just giving them the opportunity to try.

Find the Motivation

We know that motivation is a really important factor in language development and use. When supporting children with speech, language, and communication needs it is possible that we find ourselves talking for the child or trying to make things easier for them. This clearly comes from a place of 'professional love' but we must provide opportunities and motivation for children to communicate.

What really motivates the child? Is there a favourite toy, is it a certain food? Really discover what the child is interested in and then we can find ways to use this to support communication development. So, for example, you could place a favourite item in sight but out of reach. Observe the child's behaviour, how do they show you that they want the toy? Our role is then to add the words for the child – role model what they would say if they could, remembering to use single words at this stage.

The child may use a word to request the item – let's continue to repeat back what they have said so that they know they have been understood and we provide that clear speech role model.

Respond – Repeat – Extend

We are hoping that children at the start of this stage will have a vocabulary of at least 50 words and as they approach two and a half years we are hoping that they will be using short phrases and moving towards longer sentences as they approach three years of age.

By using the respond-repeat-extend strategy we can support children wherever they are in their development.

Respond – this is so important and we have discussed this is in previous chapters. Children need an interested adult to respond to them however they are communicating in order for language to develop. If you as an adult are trying to communicate with another person and they don't respond you would probably give up! We must respond! If the child is non-verbal, our response could be to mirror their play, gesture, or facial expression. This subtle act shows the child that they matter to you.

Repeat – as mentioned above, this could be to repeat the non-verbal communication, but we can also add the word that matches what the child is looking at/playing with/reaching for. When we repeat what the child has said we are modelling how the target word is said and we are confirming to the child that they have been understood. There will be times when we get this wrong and we may repeat back what we think the child has said only to be met with a look of 'that's not what I said' or the word 'no.' It is important that we are honest with children, and, if we get it wrong, it is okay to say to the child, 'I'm sorry, I got that wrong' or 'I didn't hear properly' – we are taking ownership here for the fact that we didn't understand and we are not placing any blame on the child.

If we get it wrong again it is important that we don't give up – can the child show you what they want? You can then model the word once you have identified what they have been trying to tell you.

Learning to talk can be really tricky and it is okay to say that to children if they are struggling.

Extend

This is how we can support children to move from single words to phrases and sentences.

We respond and repeat what the child has said and then we extend by adding another word. So, for example, if the child is eating a snack and says 'apple' to request more apple, the adult **responds** by offering more apple, **repeats** the child's word 'apple,' and **extends** by modelling 'more apple.' It sounds simple and easy but children need to hear these simple phrases modelled repeatedly to learn how to use them independently and then build their own phrases from their vocabulary. It is important for children to learn that these phrases can also be used in other situations and not just at the snack table, so you could use play opportunities to respond-repeat-extend to enable the child to develop phrases and sentences in a variety of different contexts.

As we extend children's language, consider what words they are already using. Have you heard any verbs (action words)? Can you introduce any verbs as you respond-repeat-extend?

Offer Strategies

We have touched on this already when we described a situation where you may need to ask a child to 'show you' what it is they want.

When a child is struggling to express themselves verbally, what other ways can they communicate what they want?

They could 'show you' – you can offer your hand and ask the child to take you to what they want.

Choices – can you narrow it down to two and ask the child 'which one?' – remembering to use the specific vocabulary when you present the choice.

Gesture/sign – the child could point to what they want and you can model the word and sign.

Use pictures – have photographs of toys/food items, can the child show you what they want by selecting the picture. You then model the vocabulary.

Be creative – what is important is that the child knows that you are interested in them and that you are doing your best to help them to communicate.

For target suggestions and interventions, see Chapter 8.

6
PRE-SCHOOLERS

Pre-school – what an amazing, adventurous time when the child will have lots of new experiences and transitions. They may also be viewed as the big girl or the big boy who will soon be going off to school. Adult expectations can grow and there is a focus on children starting to be ready for school.

Families may feel that their child should attend an early years setting full time, as many children of this age are now funded. When working with pre-school-aged children we need to reflect on the terminology we use and our expectations. By labelling children as the 'big' ones, we can add pressure to their lives without even knowing it. There are already many new things happening for them and a big change in the pace of their life is coming. Yes, we can help them get ready for this, however we must treasure their childhood and support, not push them too quickly into school life.

Now let's discover what pre-school might feel like and mean for the child. This age group is usually between three and four years old. At this stage in a child's life, being one of the younger children in the cohort can mean that your peers could be nearly a year older than you. When we look at this in terms of months on the planet and starting school, we can see that 48 months is not much time to experience the world, and neither is 60 months. However, those extra months of child development and experiences will often help the child to settle and experience transitions to school in a different way.

If we look at simple routines, such as afternoon naps, what we like to eat, and going to the toilet, there will be subtle differences for younger children. We can then examine more complex emotions of how we make friends, how we view the world, and how young children are starting to regulate their emotions and ask for help when they need it. All of these take time and practice; knowing what to do when they feel upset or angry will vary significantly in pre-school and school. Understanding how to positively communicate your needs and that sometimes these will be met with support and other times there is not an outcome that suits you is tricky.

A pre-schooler is still very young and very new to the world. There is a great deal to learn, so leaving out labels is a great help in reducing pressure. The terminology we use as adults around pre-school children can really help to build confidence for their up-and-coming transitions.

Play and the Environment

What pre-school play must be about is freedom and communication that is highly valued.

Really tapping into what will help the child now and for the future through their play – what do they love doing and how can the adult teach what is needed through this? We have mentioned the terminology used and what children hear in their everyday life. This is where your professional skills of actively listening, commenting, and interacting with children come to the forefront, by doing these you can naturally create environments of deep engagement in play.

Trust

Trusting that children know what they are doing, and as an adult in their space just being aware and interested, is enough to start with. You need to love being around the children and enabling each and every one of them to have sparks of awe and wonder every day. Imaginations need to be nurtured and grown, often this can be viewed as non-conforming behaviour, however we say take it and run with it, think about what is actually happening in the child's brain when you are teaching, is it sparking or is it switching off?

We all know what it is like to sit in a boring lesson and not take a thing in, well we certainly do not want this for young children. Pre-school children can learn so much by exploring and being adventurous. One brilliant setting we mentor calls out 'adventurers assemble' when it is time to move on. This is an exciting time of coming together and knowing the next great thing is going to happen. That next great thing could be lunchtime, where we talk, chat, laugh, enquire, discuss, and recall. Whatever opportunity we have to get to know the children and listen to their ideas is an opportunity well worth grasping.

Always remember you make the biggest difference to futures, and you are doing it right now! *'Life is what happens when you are busy making other plans'* (John Lennon). Go with what is happening right now and allow pre-school children huge chunks of time to play, then when you know how they play you can extend ideas through natural teaching moments.

Representation and Inclusion

> ### Reflection Point
>
> What we say, see, and hear changes worlds in pre-school.
>
> What do you hear yourself saying and what are the adults who work with you saying to children?
>
> What do adults say to each other in the vicinity of the children?
>
> Think about the body language you use.
>
> Think about the terminology you use.
>
> Are conversations inclusive?
>
> Do we challenge stereotypes?
>
> What do the children see in their environment and does it represent the world we live in? Not just the people in pre-school, we need to know about everyone in our world and especially about people who are marginalised and underrepresented.
>
> How is your local community represented in the pre-school? Open your doors and step out into your community, for example, what religions are there?
>
> How does pre-school help other people and create an environment where the children and the adults have theory of mind? We must be able to put ourselves in others' shoes, to know how to care about them, and understand that people in our world lead different lives from ours. What could you do to help create this pre-school environment with the children?

Play

Play is important business indeed and understanding that it is so much more than setting up an activity is crucial. Play generates how children think and make sense of their world. It introduces them to new worlds and new understanding. Play challenges our thought processes and helps create new ones. The child's comments can become the topic you decide to focus on, but we can only know this when we actively listen. We need to value play to serve as the means for dynamic insight into the child's brain development and then this development leads to the creation of the community. See we told you pre-school holds the world in its hands!

Give the children opportunities outside to explore natural resources and create on a large scale – make mixtures and create experiments. Have different terrains for them to explore, add hills, puddles, mud, digging areas, large sandpits where they can get in, small ones where they can play on their own if they want, make hidey-holes and dens. Think about the patterns of play that the children have and provide opportunities for this.

Have movable logs and tyres – a hammock and tyre swing are very easy and reasonable to make or buy. Think about how children love to move and ensure there are opportunities for this. Make sure the adults embrace this and have places where you all play and join in. Many children love running, is there a space for them to do this safely? If not, where could they do this?

Just some mud on a slight slope or some pebbles inlaid into the pavement adds another dimension to explore and comment on.

Communication
What Would We Expect to See/Hear?

By four years:

- ❖ Loads of words, approximately 1,000
- ❖ Understand adjectives (describing words), for example, 'cold,' 'soft'
- ❖ Uses words such as 'and' and 'then' to make sentences more complex
- ❖ Speech is clear and understood by most adults
- ❖ Beginning to understand language related to the concept of time, for example 'yesterday,' 'tomorrow'

Children are now using their communication skills for so many reasons, including telling simple stories and asking many, many questions. This is important as it is the way that children find out and understand more about the world around them.

Children will be communicating with their peers and using language to establish games and rules of play. As adults it is important that we allow space for children to do this but be available to model the language if needed. Not all children will develop an understanding of the social rules of play and may need adults to support them with this.

During this age range, imagination really takes off. Don't be afraid to have fun with this. You can find opportunities to introduce 'characters' to children, use funny and interesting voices for the characters in the stories you are sharing with children, create stories as you explore the outside environment – you are limited only by your own imagination.

Vocabulary

At this stage, children's vocabulary gets exciting. We are hearing a wider range of words, including adjectives (describing words) and longer, more complex sentences.

We have a role as educators to enable our children to become 'word-rich.' Expanding known vocabulary, introducing new words, describing what's happening, and making it meaningful are powerful steps towards the 'word-rich' goal.

We created a model of vocabulary teaching that helps you to reflect on your teaching and to consider if you can take vocabulary teaching one step further – bronze, silver, and gold levels of vocabulary teaching.

Imagine, you are in your outside environment and a child spots a molehill. What do you teach?

- **Bronze level** – at this level, you provide a label for the child, 'it's a molehill.' This is perfectly acceptable and if a child has severe speech and language difficulties it may be the most appropriate response.
- **Silver level** – at this level, you take it further. You label the molehill but you expand on this by considering how it got there, who or what has made it? What does a mole look like?
- **Gold level** – this is where we take things even further. You can support the child to further research the molehill, find books, search the Internet together. Could you try to replicate the molehill using natural resources? Consider the wealth of vocabulary you can be teaching as you optimise the teaching moment. You can introduce more technical vocabulary – herbivore, carnivore, foraging. Don't be afraid of these longer words, if the children are interested in their discovery let's teach them the words!

We have used molehills as an example but this same model applies to the everyday experiences that occur in early years environments.

Take a moment to think about fruit at snack time – how many of us reach 'gold level' of vocabulary teaching? Do we label the fruit? We may comment on the colour, texture, and smell. If we want to take this to 'gold' we go that step further and talk about how it grows and where it grows, we talk about climate and anti-oxidants.

Key point – it is okay not to know! It is perfectly okay if we do not know the vocabulary that takes the teaching to the gold level. Adults do not know everything and this is an important lesson for children to learn.

Learning continues for adults and if we do not have the answers or the words, we use this as a teaching moment and show the children how we can find out more. Be honest and say, 'I don't know, let's find out together.'

> **Top Tip**
>
> Support children to develop their speech, language, and communication skills without using closed questions.
>
> It can be tempting to use questions to check if a child understands or to get a response from them, but we can encourage children to talk without adding the pressure of questions, particularly closed questions.
>
> You can initiate an interaction non-verbally by establishing eye contact if the child is comfortable with that or you can position yourself next to them at the same level. You can use phrases such as 'I wonder what you are making?' that, whilst a question, does not require a response unless the child wants to offer one, therefore providing a potential conversation starter but with no pressure on the child.

Speech Sounds

We would expect children to be intelligible at this stage whilst acknowledging that there will still be some speech sound errors or difficulties.

From approximately the age of three and a half we would expect to hear words produced with final consonants and we would also expect that the processes of fronting and stopping (described in the previous chapter) to have resolved, with the child now using the sounds 'k,' 'g,' 'f,' and 's' in words.

What we might still observe is a process called weak syllable deletion, this is where the child says a multisyllabic word but misses out the quieter part of the word, for example, 'potato' would be pronounced as 'tato.'

A cluster is where two consonants are next to each other in a word, for example, '**sp**oon' as opposed to where a word starts with a consonant and then a vowel '**su**n.' It is common for children up to the age of four years to reduce these clusters to just one consonant, for example '**sp**oon' would be produced as '**p**oon.'

As we have said before, our role here is to teach by modelling. Some children during this age range may access speech and language therapy for support with their speech sounds and if you know what their tricky sounds are you can support by finding books or songs that are heavily loaded with the target sounds. This is a natural way to model the sounds that are difficult for the child without putting any pressure on them to say the sounds. Remember, they would say it if they could.

Many children will not be aware that the way they say a sound is different to you and so if we tell them they have not said it correctly or ask them to copy the way we say the sound, this can be frustrating, confusing, and upsetting for the child.

The Role of the Educator – Adult-Child Interaction

Let's take a moment to reflect…

Let's discover the adult's key role when working with pre-school children. Children observe, watch, learn, and copy from the people in their life, and as their educator you will be one of these main people. Pre-school children have an amazing ability to copy what they see; it is their world around them that influences their play. At times at this age their communication is shaped by what they see and hear and by who surrounds them. Quite often this is the age when the children will literally copy what you say. Role play can often demonstrate how they view their world and how they are learning to interact with others.

Being mindful of the terminology we use and our actions is part of robust practice in early years. The adults around pre-schoolers must always think about what they say and what they do with young children. Reflecting on how your actions affect others is a key message for all adults to know about themselves and to also teach the children. We have discussed the power dynamic and the need for children to have power over their own lives, with this age group of children this becomes of paramount importance. They are getting ready to move on to another phase of their lives, adults who support this transitional phase robustly and with kindness can enable children to feel confident and enjoy future learning.

Transition to School

How can educators and adults help to smooth the way to school and embed a love of future lifelong learning well?

We can do this through supporting children and giving plenty of time for transitions, really knowing each child and what their likes and dislikes are and ensuring that this information is shared often with their families and built upon. When it is time for transition reports, gaining as much information of the child at home and at the setting will really help to enable their new teacher to know the child well and to help them to settle.

There should be no surprises for families in a transitional report. If educators have concerns about a child, these should be shared with the family as they occur; everyone can then work together and continue to be a valued and interactive part in the child's community of care, love, and education. Conversations with families can sometimes be a bit tricky. Building foundations of open and honest dialogue from the family's initial visit is a great place to start, so mention that if you have any concerns you will communicate with them. Equally if the family has any concerns ensure that they know you are willing to listen, help, and signpost where needed.

What works well in a pre-school and what do educators/adults need to be mindful of?

Offering many new open-ended experiences, listening to the children's ideas especially around role play, and facilitating these by having resources handy that the children can use.

The idea here is for the children to take ownership of their play and the adult helping and offering provocation when required. It isn't for us to take their idea and run with it. For example, a child observes an aeroplane in the sky, the adults make an aeroplane, and the children come in and play with it. There is a subtle difference in children creating what they are thinking and the educator supporting this. Yes, add provocation and ideas when invited; however, do not take it on as a military project with a picture in mind of how perfect it will look. The process and the learning that takes place along the way are the finest teaching and learning moments, when we trust the pre-school children they can then become dynamic learners in charge of their own destiny and the adults will probably learn a thing or two along the way.

Autonomy

The children require autonomy and space to think in their play, especially when making independent decisions. They will communicate to you if they need the help of an adult. Think about the ways that children communicate and ensure adults are observing all communications and not just verbal cues.

Reflection Point

Making independent decisions and choices:

- ❖ Do the adults do most of the thinking for the children?
- ❖ How are the children listened to throughout the day and what happens if they want to change the routine?
- ❖ Independence: Are there times throughout the day where you can naturally replicate what might happen in the school day?
- ❖ For instance, think about snack time at school, what will the children need to do for themselves and what does snack time really look like for a young child at school? Can you bring elements of this into your practice?
- ❖ Often school snack is running around the playground with their friends and eating an apple or banana on the go. How can you teach these everyday skills they will need? Think about safety, think about the ratio of adults to children in school.
- ❖ How will you know that when the pre-school cohort of children go to school, they will be independent and self-assured?
- ❖ Will the children ask for help when they need it?
- ❖ Will they know how to wait if their needs are not initially met, and will they be confident to ask someone else to help them?
- ❖ How will you and your team have enabled them to have easier real-life transitions?
- ❖ Break down the everyday and look at the similarities of being in early years and the transitions to school.
- ❖ Do we feel that children who have had freedom will not be able to sit down and listen? Getting children school ready does not mean that you teach them to conform, it means you help them to thrive, explore, have adventures, and question, and you find exciting ways to help them listen and be calm through their child-led interests. For example, if a child is interested in cars and she is enabled to play with these in many areas, how much longer might she concentrate on her own play and ideas? Having cars in the sand, water, paint, and mud means she could access more of her desired play and be deeply engaged in her ideas. Supported by an adult who really observes and extends interests well and knows when to give autonomy, the child could easily sit, stand, and crouch for long periods of time.
- ❖ When we tap into child-led interests this can extend the child's deep enjoyment and engagement in play. It also fits into what children really need for their pre-school year, longer periods of uninterrupted concentration, with teachers/adults who know when to add provocation, when to comment, and when to extend play.

> ❖ Helping young children to embrace change can only be achieved when they are in an environment that supports this; the adults in the environment will need to view change as a positive way forward.

Our lives constantly change, though we may set out thinking we know what will happen today; however, as adults and children we will need to understand and embrace the idea that life is constantly changing and has ups and downs. If we are looking for constant security, where things stay the same and where we try to control outcomes, then we will have done ourselves and the children a disservice.

Incorporate change into practice and work with what you have today, grasp the opportunity where the children understand that everyday transitions happen often and do not create an event around these or school transition, just build little steps every day that enable children to thrive now and in their futures.

Having said all this, we must not just focus on transitions and what we believe the school will want. We need to think about the child really growing and extending their knowledge through rich moments and valued play. Pre-school is a time to embrace childhood and non-conformity. It is a beautiful time in a child's life of fun, mud, freedom, running wild and climbing trees, of snuggling up and having all the time in the world to create stories and develop imaginations where nothing is impossible. Treasuring this time with the children is what pre-school in early years is all about. There will be plenty of time in later years where what the child has learned with you will enable them to bounce back and be who they really need to be.

Think about the amazing people who have enabled you as you grew to have fun times filled with love, laughter, awe, and wonder and to know that your emotions are valid. Now go out and discover these again and again with the children you work with. If you did not have people in your life who helped to create these moments, then think of the people whose actions you would change and how differently you will teach. Reframing our thinking and embracing change helps us to teach young children.

Small Group Time

This is often something that adults in early years feel that they must do in the pre-school years. We must always question why we practice as we do. Why do we ask children to come together and perform in front of each other? Is this an enjoyable experience for the children? It could be. Is it natural in everyday life to do this? What would the adults feel like if they were asked to do this daily? Is there a real depth of learning and development happening or could this be achieved through natural play choices and tuned in adults?

Whose Agenda Is It?

Is it a fun teaching moment where all the children are involved or is it something that has always been done? Really look at the children's communication through their body language, what are they telling you?

Are the children really engaged in the process or are they just waiting for a turn? If the end goal is to enable children to sit and wait, there are far better ways of enabling this through play. Question how you can cover all the children's requirements in a small group time? What do you really want them to learn? What other ways will they learn this? The majority of adults will be able to sit and listen when they are older when they need to; it is not really a skill to be held accountable for or to be celebrated. It is not how children learn; children are not passive learners! They are bouncy, loud, quiet, energetic, snuggling types of learners who can embrace learning through play. Reflect on what you believe children should learn and why, and look at further research on how children learn.

Always understand your practice first before jumping in to teach children. Remember just because that is how it was done or has always been done is not researched practice. To build future brains we must research and actively listen.

Think about natural times of the day when children come together where adults can support the children's life skills, such as hand washing, putting coats on, putting shoes on, eating times. There are many times throughout the day that have amazing opportunities for teaching children new skills and enhancing communication. Generating a small group time to test children's learning is not necessary. Bringing everyone together and halting play is not necessary. Understanding how children learn is vital, and understanding how each child learns is critical. Think of yourself as a brain-scientist or brain-builder, we all have different paths and individual lives to lead. You are an important teacher who facilitates brain development.

Having opportunities where children come together will happen naturally with the right environment of learning. Children will lead games and you can support this and enhance learning naturally.

The Physical Environment and Small Group Time

Often pre-school small group times are used for school readiness, so here is where we need to mention school readiness for the pre-schoolers. We can hear you shouting back at us: 'but is the school ready for the children?' and rightly so! The answer to this is we do not know without the background information of what every feeder school and reception class is like. Building robust connections with the schools the children will move on to is key and doing this from the beginning of the new term (basically at least nine months before children go to school) really helps your setting, the children and the families know what to expect. Now some schools will value this and welcome you with open arms. They will know the foundations that you are putting in place will enable children to thrive in their new physical environment and with them. They will understand that professional early years practice holds the key to successful transitions and a love of lifelong learning.

Here it is best to mention that early years providers can only work with what they have, we are a brilliant sector for creating networking, and being particularly creative with ideas and processes. Hold on to that and know you are doing your best for the families who choose to place their pre-schoolers with you.

Your local school is a bit too busy to help:

If you or one of your colleagues know of a reception teacher, headteacher, or a member of the local school who is particularly dynamic then asking them to speak to your network of early years could really help gain information on transitions for many children. Adults in early years are advocates for all children and the more information we share and gain the better we develop our early years practice and wider professionalism. The more knowledge we can gain from what it really feels like to be in school the better we can support the child's transition.

Reflection Point

What do we really need to know about our own physical environments and schools' physical environments that will help pre-school children to settle?

- ❖ What does this new physical environment feel and look like? Planning this with an initial visit to each school from you and your team in pre-school will really help. We know this could be time-consuming, however it will be time well spent and you will be able to support the children well, with real-life thoughts and ideas.
- ❖ Visit all the local schools that the children will attend to create communications and understanding.
- ❖ Create a photo book with the children at your setting of the local schools.
- ❖ Can you visit and use the playground or field? Start to see, hear, and be part of the environment as the norm (we know you probably can't go every day, and you might get in the way of school life).
- ❖ Make sure your community walks go past schools at busy playtimes so that the children experience the noises.
- ❖ Bring in PE kits in a named bag and see who wants to get involved in this.
- ❖ Use utensils in play and supported by an adult – making and cutting sandwiches are skills that will help.

Pre-Schoolers

- ❖ Have words around them that mean something to them.
- ❖ If they are interested in letters, support this with sticks, sand trays, magnets, pens, paint, chalk. Go big first as children need to use their large muscles from their shoulders and arms to be able to even think about holding a pen.
- ❖ Remember it is not the early years mission to make children hold pens and write their names.
- ❖ We can introduce phonics if children are really interested and this is done naturally in practice, not sat down with flashcards. Go on a walk and look out for text such as road signs and names of places. Meaningful physical environments that children are interested in is key.
- ❖ Are children able to listen? Are the adults who support them able to listen and respond. There are many ways of enabling listening through child-led play. Outside is particularly great for this.
- ❖ Again, this is not a setup, sit-down activity; rather, this is a time when you may be outside and you hear something, such as a bird, and you point this out to the children close by. You might all choose to go on a listening walk and talk about what you all hear in the moment as you hear. If children decide to progress further and are really interested in writing and reading, you support them to do this.
- ❖ Are there opportunities for children to tell stories to each other?
- ❖ We need to know that children will require many independent skills and this comes through having the time to practice and develop these.
- ❖ Have you also thought about adding photographs of the teachers and other adults from the schools the children will attend to your family wall next to a photo of the school? Seeing these in the everyday will really help. Typically, you would have your photos on the family wall from the first day next to a photo of your setting and talk about building communities. This is the child's wider family and to see this makes a positive difference in building connections.
- ❖ Building communications: Have natural conversations with the children as they are playing around their thoughts about going to school. Let them know that you were little and you went to school, how did it feel for you?

Small group times: Let's change things up a bit, let's use this time for trying out new skills such as taking shoes and socks off and on, putting pumps on, changing into shorts, and practising many more everyday occurrences that could really help the child to gain new emotional and physical skills that they need when starting school. Use this valuable time to explore the community and create real-life maps of where you live and what is important to the children.

The Role of the Educator – Small Group Time

Small group time – it is vital to understand and reflect on what the educator's/adult's role is.

> ### Reflection Point
>
> Think about teaching pre-school children within small groups:
>
> - Offer a small group, never enforce it.
> - What is the adult wanting to teach the children?
> - Does the adult know why they want to teach this?
> - Does the adult think all the children will engage and if not, how will you engage children in a different way?
> - Is the adult doing most of the talking?
> - Is the adult carrying out most of the activity?
> - Has the adult got an end product in mind? If the answer is yes, what happens if children have different ideas?
> - Does the adult take account of children's different learning styles?
> - Is the process respected and the outcome adjusted and re-focused depending on how individual children respond?
> - Is the adult reading, noting, and responding to children's body language?
> - How does the adult know that the children are deeply engaged?
> - What might be a natural time of the day for this focus?
> - Do the environments vary for small group time?
> - Where else could you teach that would be inspiring for the children?
> - Do children have to sit down to learn?
> - Do children have to sit in a circle to learn?
> - Depending on levels of interactions and interests can the activity be stopped and children go to play?
> - Can the activity be open-ended, or will the time allowance mean that the adult will need to stop even if the children are really engaged?
>
> Evaluating small group time honestly is key; were all children really engaged, enabled to ask questions, and were they really involved? Is this the best way to teach? Did it have meaning for the children or was everyone going through the motions? What was the adult's role and how did the session make the children and adults feel?

Pre-Schoolers

Children Were all of them...	Adult Teaching had...	What could the adult do differently next time?	What did the atmosphere in this session feel like? Where next?
Deeply engaged	Deep levels of engagement		
Enabled to ask questions	Awe and wonder		
Enabled to talk and enquire	Inspiration and respect for the children		
Listened to, including body language	Time and flexibility		
Considered in their learning process	Positive body language to match activity		

- ❖ Ensure if you carry out small group time that it is a place to thrive and not fail for children.
- ❖ Do not compare children.
- ❖ Do not put children on the spot.
- ❖ Respect the quiet children and find another way to communicate with them.
- ❖ Remember children learn when they feel emotionally secure.

Families and Small Group Time

Ensuring families are involved in their child's learning is crucial, and telling them about their child's day in pre-school and the skills they are developing really helps families to understand what life is like for their child in pre-school. What could families help their children with that is not time consuming or onerous in their busy lives? How could they help their children to develop and how could you help the families to understand that they are fundamental to their child's learning? Individuals in families have not always had the best time in school and may think they cannot help teach their own children. Tap into the family's individual skills, what could they teach the children? Inviting them in for small group times will enhance the experience and widen everyone's thoughts and ideas.

Expectations

Should we sit and write at small group time? Have resources all around where the children can express themselves, mark, make, and write in their everyday play and ensure the children see different texts throughout their environment. The children and adults could also create a writing area for a purpose, such as an office or a doctor's surgery, pizza restaurant, shop, deli, and many more ideas. Also ask the parents what are the children interested in and how can you support this? What do they see and do on their journey to the setting and what do they see and do in their local community? Replicating this will have far more meaning for the children.

Many families may worry that children should be writing and reading before school; now there may be children who are interested in this, however it is not the role of the educator in pre-schools to ensure that all children do this. Sharing with parents how you are helping children to develop their skills to get ready and build the foundations of the fine motor skills that children will need for later life and for writing is a great way forward.

Holding a family evening at the start of a new term to explain all about the early years curriculum and how and why they play a key role in their child's educational journey often works well. As educators you will come across many family worries and questions about the early years that need unpicking, explaining, and supporting. You are the professional in the early years field and can share new knowledge and researched evidence. Sharing your expertise and research behind pre-school practice can enable families to gain trust in the processes and the ethos of the setting. This does not mean that the adults in pre-school need to know everything about early years, no one knows everything. It means adults will communicate that they are not quite sure, however they will find someone or something that does help answer the question or query. Signposting and collaborating with other professionals who can help is an important role for early years educators to embrace.

Including families in small group storytimes, especially adults who speak languages that the children may not have heard, can be a really positive experience. For the child to hear their significant adult from their family reading to the children gives a great sense of belonging, and tapping into their skills and hobbies really helps strengthen the community you are all creating. When families feel welcome and understand what you do their respect and involvement grow. Equally when early educators really involve families, mutual respect and understanding develop. This does not mean you will think in the same way or even have the same values, it means you respect others' opinions and life choices and they respect yours.

As we have mentioned, everyone feels that they know how to raise children because of their experiences of being a child. They may choose to parent in a way totally different from their own childhood or they may decide their childhood was fine and that it is good to parent the way they were brought up. The influences of significant adults in our lives resonate throughout our early years practice and child-rearing.

To understand more than just what we know to be right for us we must research, read, and extend our knowledge of child development, emotional regulation with co-regulation, and the child's brain development. Above all else we must listen to the child however they decide to communicate and advocate with and for them. Be the early years educator who enhances lives daily and observe what happens when you really listen.

Communication
Vocabulary Boost – Small Group Time

Small group time can be a part of the day that you have organised and planned for but it can also be those incidental moments when you find yourself with a small group of children who have naturally been drawn together through a common interest – this could be an interesting find in the outdoor environment or that they were all hungry and arrived for a snack at the same time.

These small group moments are such a good opportunity for building relationships and extending language skills. You may find that there are some children who feel more confident to express themselves in small groups rather than in a whole group situation.

Small group situations provide a great opportunity for meaningful conversations. As an adult, you can support the children's understanding of the social rules of conversation – turn-taking, waiting for the other person to finish talking before you start, and also being aware of the interest of the listener and knowing when to stop talking.

Books

Books can be a really useful resource to share with a small group of children. The benefits of reading to children have been widely documented but the key points are:

- Introducing new vocabulary.
- Engaging a child's imagination which may then stimulate imaginative play (an important way that children learn about the world).
- Role modelling how we say words – how sounds blend together to form words and how we change our tone of voice to add 'stress' to important words.
- There may be times when as adults we are unsure of how to read a certain word, and this provides the opportunity to model how we break the word down into 'chunks' or sounds as we try to work out how to say it – think dinosaur names!
- Role modelling pace – giving the child the opportunity to hear how we pause at the end of sentences or when introducing a new idea.

When we share books with small groups of children we can support meaningful, natural conversation about the story. We can extend children's thoughts and ideas and in a smaller group children will have a greater opportunity to express themselves, and the adults have more time to respond.

Books enable children to develop an interest in fictional characters and their emotions, and they can also provide an opportunity to learn about cultures different from the child's.

You can take this to another level by creating an atmosphere of storytelling. Use your imagination to create stories that you share with children and you can support children to share their thoughts and ideas about their play and enable them to create their own stories.

As imagination develops so does the wealth of words a child will experience and then use.

Key point – Whilst some children may feel more confident to express themselves in a small group, some children may still find this difficult or overwhelming. If you observe a child who appears uncomfortable talking in front of others, find ways that the child can join in without having to speak – this could be through something physical such as dancing, joining in actions to songs, or finding props which link with the book you are sharing. What is important is that the child feels part of their community and that they are valued.

Speech Sound Boost – Small Group Time

As we mentioned in Chapter 4, phonological awareness refers to an understanding that sets of sounds combine together to make words and requires knowledge of rhyme, syllable awareness, and the ability to hear and then produce the beginning and end of words.

With our pre-school children we can support speech sound development by raising awareness of sounds and how we produce them.

Small group time is about sharing an interest together and, as we mentioned earlier, this can be planned or totally 'in the moment.' As we talk and extend children's ideas, we can start to raise awareness of how a word 'sounds.' We can talk about the sound at the start of the word and discover if we know any other words that start with that sound. We can explore what is happening in our mouth as we say that sound – are our lips moving? Is our tongue moving? Is it a loud sound or a quiet sound? Is it a long or short sound?

We can use small group time to introduce the idea that words are made up of syllables. Don't be afraid to introduce this word, we can add an explanation that syllables are the beats to a word and we can clap them as we say the word or we can bang a drum with every 'beat.'

We can talk about words which rhyme (sound almost the same). Can we think of any more words that rhyme? Do we know any songs or books with lots of rhyme? Can we make up funny words which rhyme with our names?

Have fun with sounds and words!

Speech, Language, and Communication Needs

When/how would we know if a child was struggling with their communication?

Look

- ❖ Can the child follow instructions containing at least three keywords? 'Put the <u>spoon</u> <u>under</u> the <u>box</u>' – where there is an alternative to spoon, under, and box.
- ❖ Is the child developing relationships with peers or are they still playing alongside others or on their own?

Listen

- ❖ Is the child difficult to understand?
- ❖ Is the child able to put their thoughts and ideas into sentences?
- ❖ Is the child's talking bumpy and dysfluent, with pauses and/or frequent repetitions of whole words or parts of words?
- ❖ Is the child taking turns in conversation?

Learn

Children need to be able to follow longer instructions to access the early years curriculum and to develop their language skills. They need a large and varied vocabulary to express their thoughts and ideas.

Children who are not yet interacting with their peers or who become distressed when other children approach them will have fewer opportunities to develop social interaction skills and develop friendships and are then at risk of social isolation.

At this age we would expect children to be generally fluent and intelligible; if we are observing that the child is struggling to be understood or that their talking is bumpy and dysfluent (frequent repetitions of sounds or whole words, stretching of sounds typically at the start of words, or long pauses whilst going red in the face when trying to say a word), we need to seek advice from a speech and language therapist. We need to support the child with their emotions and it is okay to acknowledge that learning to talk can be tricky.

HOW CAN WE SUPPORT THE CHILD WITH SPEECH, LANGUAGE, AND COMMUNICATION NEEDS?

Practitioner Toolkit

- Time-space-pace
- Be interested
- Positive body language

Time-Space-Pace

We may have identified that the child needs support to develop their communication skills, but we must resist the urge to 'take over' their play. They still have their own ideas and need to play and explore in a way that is meaningful to them. Our role is to give the child **space** to be themselves, join the play if invited, wait for the child to start talking (**time**), and then when we respond, be aware of the language load and the processing time needed by the child (**pace**).

Time-space-pace is a strategy that can be used with all children as it creates a communication environment of observation and listening as well as a calm atmosphere.

Be Interested

If a child does invite you to join them – this may be verbally but this may be a more subtle invitation through eye contact or body language, be interested in what they are showing you or telling you.

Children can be good at observing body language, facial expression, and tone of voice – they will know if you are not really 'present.' By showing genuine interest in the child and their play and ideas, the child is going to be more motivated to engage. The more engagement we achieve, the greater the opportunity for teaching vocabulary and the 'rules' of conversation – taking turns, answering questions, asking questions, making eye contact, and understanding facial expressions.

When a child is interested in something and we share that interest with them, we are given the opportunity to extend language and introduce new ideas and concepts.

Positive Body Language

We have mentioned this already but it is so important that our facial expression and body language 'match' the verbal message we are communicating; if not, it will be very confusing for the child with language difficulties. If we look 'cross' a child will notice this and it is likely to create a feeling of worry for the child. Remember, if a child is not feeling safe and secure, they cannot learn and develop as their brain goes into a state of 'fight, flight or freeze' and is more concerned with feeling safe rather than listening to what we are saying or showing them.

When we 'connect' with a child the child learns that we are interested in them and they are more likely to engage and then learn. Keeping our body language open, relaxed, and calm is a good way to enable the child to connect with us.

For specific target suggestions, see Chapter 8.

7
TRANSITIONS INTO SCHOOL

Transitions into school from early years always seem to feel very big – so how can we prepare for this in order for it to be fluid, successful, and truly understood? The impact of early transitions is the foundation of where we start to embrace change. When adults talk about the big school to the child and talk to them about being grown up, we wonder: how does this make children feel?

If transitioning to school was viewed as just the next step, a place where children can still play and have their interests and ideas reflected in their new environment, this might be a whole lot easier for them. The way all significant adults talk about moments in children's lives has a huge impact on how the child views their experiences and the world around them.

> **Reflection Point**
>
> **Barriers to Transitions**
>
> Have a think for a moment: How do you feel as an adult when you start a new job, attend an interview, meet a new visitor at your setting, or even catch up with a relative. What might you do to prepare for this?
>
> Now let us add the next layer of thought, what if when you started to prepare for an interview everyone commented, 'this is you, going into the big league now,' 'you will need to be a big person to fit in here,' and then took lots of photographs of you, what might you feel like? Now remember as an adult you have a choice you do not need to go; you can stay where you feel comfortable and settled and where everyone knows your name. We can start to see from this how the children's transition might feel and why they may become upset and anxious.

DOI: 10.4324/9781003139829-8

We do understand that adults are trying to be supportive and make it all sound exciting; however, there needs to be careful consideration around what we say to children. Enabling choice and working with the child to really understand how they feel is paramount. Transitions should never feel 'done to' the child. We will explore more on this reflective consideration later in this chapter, for now just hold that thought in mind.

Transitions are an ongoing progression in life. We learn to manage and hopefully embrace them when we have supportive foundations in place. We want children to go running into the next chapter of their life with huge confidence and self-esteem. We want them to know that they are kept in mind. However, we do not want to hold them back, we have hopefully taught them well and supported them to know that they matter, that they are secure and can explore and start to thrive in a different environment. We want to enable children to see change as a positive aspect in their lives. So let us discover how we learn to embrace transitions and how to enable 'school readiness.' This is not a term we like; however, it is a well-known term, and this terminology should be explored further.

School Readiness – What Does This Mean for the Child?

Now when we talk about school readiness, we seem to forget that the child has already transitioned many times before they get to school. As babies many children are cared for by extended families and friends, they may have attended early years provisions, toddler groups, played at friends' houses, and gone on holiday. Many children will be living in two homes, transitioning weekly.

By thinking about and understanding the child's lived experiences, we can often see how much support and reassurance a child needs to feel secure when away from their family. Talking with their family and valuing what they know about their child and their routines is fundamental. Every child is unique! We hear this a lot, but what does it actually mean for every individual child you work with? Do you know and understand the child's life experiences, do you know what happens in their life when they are not with you? Can you help them to feel understood, do you create environments where they have ownership and can express themselves? Knowing that we are safe to express emotions is a key element of transitions. Belonging and having a strong sense of self will really help, as a professional we can help by having robust professional attachments with the child and ensuring they always feel 'kept in mind.' If a child knows you think about them when they are not with you, then they will know you have not forgotten them when they move on to the next phase of their educational journey.

> **Reflection Point**
>
> Think back to the scenario of the job interview, did you speak to a friend to tell them how you felt? Did they help to reassure you and listen to how you felt?
>
> You are one of the child's biggest allies in settling and transitioning for the child, you are their friend, you have got them, you understand how they feel, you have theory of mind, you can put yourself in the child's shoes and really understand how they are and what it would be like for them. Discover what makes each child feel safe and understood, share, and build upon this information as the foundation of each transition. Transitions are an individual journey for each and every one of us. The key is to unpick this and build upon strengths and support journeys of development.

Attachment-Led Practice

In early years, attachment-led practice is fundamental from the moment a child starts a new provision; this enables the child to feel understood and listened to, and it leads to brighter futures for secure, engaged children with robust self-esteem. Work at the child's pace in all transitions, observe and understand their gestures and body language, ensure that they are shown that they really do matter and are safe. Foundational education and teaching in early years are amazing; as practitioners, we really can help enable children to have the best start in life. We do not want to rush this; remember that a child's learning happens every moment, the skill of the practitioner is to trust the child, know when to extend, when to give time and space. Now we could argue that families and busy early years provisions do not have time to settle children at an individual pace. However, we would then need to question how do children learn? Yes, you are right children, and adults for that matter, can only learn when they are secure, and their personal, social, and emotional needs are met. As professionals in early years we know that spending the time at the very start and foundation of a child's educational journey will then help to enable them to have easier, successful transitions in all areas of their life.

Routines

Everyday routines in early years are the key to robust transitions to school. Have a look at the following list and reflect on the points.

- ❖ Do your routines enable children to thrive?
- ❖ Are your routines attachment led and flexible?
- ❖ Do they account for individual ideas from the children?
- ❖ Do your routines promote confidence or just conformity?

- Is the child's voice heard and is it listened to in everyday routines?
- Did the children help make the routines and do they have ownership of them (a great way to promote independent skills and critical thinking skills)?
- Are children's own routines respected?
- Is each child treated equally and is this reflected in your environment?
- Do your routines reflect each child and the way they choose to communicate.

Think about what really must be done each day, such as registrations, eating times, and toileting, and see what flexibility and teaching can be brought into these elements. Remember eating times can be one of the most wonderful experiences for children and adults to sit down together and really take time to get to know each other. They can also be a battlefield of negativity and this is not good for anyone's self-esteem. Transitioning from playing to sitting down and eating needs careful planning and understanding, always ensure that children have ownership of this and that you treasure these moments with them. Do not be the food warden, children will eat when they are hungry and if they are full, they will stop. Never tell a child to eat up all their dinner, and don't offer rewards for eating or take away puddings for not eating. The dinner is the treat, let them move on when they are ready; when their brains are telling them they are full, respect this. Children can control only two things in life: their eating and their toileting. As adults, by understanding and respecting this you are enabling the children to have power in their own lives, something they will need as they transition through life.

Reflection Point

Transition Objects

When a child brings something from home this is important to them, it is a piece of familiarity and may mean the difference between settling or being worried and sad. Children must be able to see themselves in their environment. We know it is difficult if every child brings something in, as it may get lost or another child might want to play with it. However, we do need to think about what it means to the child. There are many ways to have a happy medium of understanding, and developing fair rules and boundaries with the children and families is key. For example, you may not want a certain toy being brought in, the child could have a photo of themselves with it and this could be kept wherever the child can easily access it.

Photograph books and family displays really help children to see themselves in their environment. A photo of when a family member returns to pick up provides visual evidence for the child that someone always comes back for them, and when they see themselves in their environment, they know that they matter.

We are also not the dummy monitors, if a child needs a soother of any kind to feel safe, we cannot be the person to take this away from them. We can work with the child and family around this and progress at the child's pace.

It often helps to think about how transitions feel for the child; imagine going to an appointment and as you turn up the receptionist takes your phone, bag, drink, purse, and notes you had made, then pops then on the highest shelf so that if you want them you must ask. Would that help you to stay connected and feel safe to explore?

School Readiness and Are They School Ready?

Now we can progress on to being ready for school, or as most early years professionals say, 'are they school ready'? There is responsibility for the school where the children are transitioning to, to work with the children, families, and early years professionals to enable the best transition for each child. Each school has an individual identity and the more we understand this the easier transitions will be for the children.

By the age of four or five the child will now hopefully understand that someone who loves them always comes back for them at the end of their day. They know they are kept in mind by a significant person in their life. If a child is anxious about being left it is especially important to contain their feelings and take whatever positive steps are needed to help them; involve their family with this. Never rush a transition, as we know this is the building block for foundations of confidence and a child's voice being heard. It is integral to enabling positive school transitions that every transition is natural and at the child's pace.

Always ask yourself: where is the child in all of this? Where is their point of view?

This is the beginning of a journey throughout the child's life, to demystify what happens and to help children prepare for change in their future life is crucial. For this we will need to use theory of mind, take a step back, and be invited into the individual and unique child's world.

What Is the Role of the Early Years Practitioner in Transitions?

Our role in early years is to be one of support, understanding, and subtle preparation. Transitions will always be a smoother journey if they are introduced through play. As we have mentioned, they will naturally occur throughout life.

So what could we do in practice that would really help? Naming emotions and talking about these from birth with children is key to the child understanding how they feel and in starting to develop emotional intelligence. If a child is crying, to say to them you look sad and empathise with them enables them to understand you are interested and they are worth caring about. We could say, 'come on, stop crying, you are okay.' However well-meant this is, it does not help the child to feel understood. We are in a privileged position of teaching children and enhancing brain development. To teach a child to express how they are feeling and share this is crucial for their future well-being.

School transitions need to be in place naturally from the start of early years. Great resources around this can be photograph books of your community and amongst these will be the local schools and schools that children are going to attend. School readiness resources should be local and meaningful to the child. School uniforms, book bags, and PE clothes and pumps in the role play areas really help (all of this can be free and donated from older siblings). If we look at snack times at school what happens? We have found that children tend to have their own snack and bottle, which are named, and they help themselves to it. If you think about children at school, they are usually in the playground running around and stopping to have a bite of their apple or share something with their friends. The more we can support children to be independent (children are extremely capable), the easier their transition will be. A great way to embrace what happens at school is to think about the whole school day and work out what skill you think children will need. There is a note of caution here, sitting down and writing should not be one of these, we are embedded in early years and we all know children learn through play and through our skill at extending this and their ideas.

Children in the early years do not learn by sitting down and being made to carry out an activity. Children may naturally squat or lay on the floor for exceptionally long periods of time if they are deeply engaged and interested. Mark-making areas inside and outside, large physical movements, balancing, and materials that can be manipulated, such as playdough and clay are how children in early years start to build muscles and create gross and fine motor skills. There are endless ways to enable pre-writing in early years that follow children's interests. Remember that children's hands and fingers are not yet ready to write at this young age. However, if a child is really interested in writing, then we would extend and support this.

Reading a story is fabulous if the child is really interested in it; however, not all children will be interested at the same time. Yes, we know that in some reception classes this is asked as a skill when children arrive at school. However, we must then question whether this constitutes being 'school ready.' Children will sit down and listen when they are engaged and interested. Most adults can sit down and many do sit down all day for work, so it isn't really a skill that needs to be mastered at such a young age. So many amazing schools now embrace continual provision and have specialised early years teachers. We must work with the best of the research in early years and not with outdated ideas. As an early year's advocate spreading this word, backed up by research, your input can become part of conversations and connections with local schools.

Early years is a professional body of teachers of which you are an integral part. Knowing children individually is a real skill and understanding what enables their interest to grow and how the child learns is what should be shared with the child's new teacher.

> **Reflection Point**
>
> When you have looked at routines in school, what have you decided is different? What can you do to help prepare the child for this?
>
> Whatever you decide to do, make it fun and interesting and resist the urge to say in 'big school you will...'
>
> A great way to start a conversation with the children is, 'I wonder what happens in school?'
>
> This is good to gauge how much life experience each child has of school. If they have an older sibling and go to pick them up from school, then they may know the routines and the environment well. You could ask this child and their family if they would take some photographs for you to share and this will promote further discussions.
>
> The following points can be helpful to prepare for school transitions:
>
> - Talking naturally with children in everyday conversations about school.
> - Having registers in the writing area and modelling this play.
> - PE clothes and pumps in the dressing up area.
> - Individual named drinks and snacks that the children can help themselves to at snack time.
> - Book bags with whatever the children feel they want to put in and share.
> - Looking at school websites together; often there will be photos of the principal.
> - Photos of schools in your community.
> - Photos of teachers at those schools.
> - Walks that take you and the children past these schools.
> - School visits to play in the playground or fields.

- ❖ Teacher visits to your setting – remember to keep this natural and the teacher can just be around and say hello.
- ❖ Homemade books about going to school and leaving the early years provision.
- ❖ Small world – school resources.
- ❖ Model building provocation 'I was thinking of building a school,' 'I wonder what is in a school'? some children will be interested and some will not – this is an activity that children choose to take part in.
- ❖ Validate how the child feels, talk about this and share with families.
- ❖ Ask children to wear school uniforms in the last term before leaving your setting, if they want to and make sure they can play in it; explain to families it will get dirty and will get paint on, etc. The idea here is that you are bringing a school uniform into the everyday and demystifying it. Keeping a school uniform for best and hung up ready for the 'big day' will not help ease any worries.
- ❖ Homemade books around starting school made with the children.
- ❖ Reading books about school together at the child's pace.
- ❖ Naming emotions in everyday play and using this knowledge to see how the child feels about starting school.
- ❖ Mentioning school naturally in conversations and observing children's gestures and demeanours. Gain deeper knowledge and understanding of how each child feels. You can then plan, use provocation, and extend the child's experiences.

Reflection Point

Remember to use positive language around transition and share this with families.

Be really prepared; as soon as a child starts their last academic year with you, hold a family's evening right at the start of this term around 'transitions to school and school readiness.' Share the information in this chapter and make it clear that the families are integral to brighter futures for their child.

Just a Few Things Not to Say

Well, you will not be able to do that at school.

When you are a big school 'boy' or 'girl' you will have to sit still.

Make sure you keep your uniform clean.

Listen to your teacher and do as you are told. *Does this seem controversial?*

If we reflect a little deeper and look at how children learn and why we are sending them to be educated it becomes clearer. Children create the future of our society. Yes, they will need to be polite; however, this does not mean agreeing with everything a figure of authority says to them. Children should be taught to think for themselves, to listen to others, and to have their own views. Independence, creativity, and a love of lifelong learning do not come from just being told what to do. It comes from experiencing life and education in the real world. Educating a child to know that their voice is heard, and that they are integral to their own journey, is crucial.

Children will need to be critical thinkers on their own educational paths. As educationists we all want the child to grow and to continue to be a dynamic person in their wider community, a person who has the ability to make and embrace change. We need children to excel past what we know and teach them, grow their own minds, and create a world of which they are proud to be an integral part.

As you can see, school transitions really are an integral part of a lifelong journey for the child.

HOW CAN WE SUPPORT THE CHILD WITH SPEECH, LANGUAGE, AND COMMUNICATION NEEDS?

Is there anything else as early years professionals we can do to support a smooth and comfortable transition into school for children who are struggling to communicate?

We have a duty of care to these children to ensure that the adults who will be educating them at this next stage of their education journey are aware of how the child is communicating, what barriers they face, and what they need to help them to communicate effectively.

You may have heard of a 'communication passport,' but we feel that this terminology indicates that the child needs this document in order to *gain access* to their new learning environment and so we prefer to use a 'This is Me' document.

The aim of the 'This is Me' document is to empower children and help to inform the 'reader' of the child's life and personality.

This document 'belongs' to the child, it gives them a voice to share key information about themselves and should therefore be written in the first person.

This template has suggested headings that you may find useful but feel free to amend the headings to best suit the child.

Transitions into School

'This Is Me' Template

| I live with: | This is me: | My friends are: |

| Things that make me happy: | Other important people in my life: | Things that make me sad: |

| When I am happy I: | Important things in my life: (hobbies/interests/pets) |

| Information relating to general health: | Things that might worry me: |

This is how I communicate:

| These people help me: | Self-care skills: | Religion/other cultural things that are important to me: |

Information relating to general health:

thriving Language

8
SPEECH, LANGUAGE, AND COMMUNICATION NEEDS

What Are Speech, Language, and Communication Needs?

Everyone with speech, language, and communication needs is unique and will present differently. You may see two children with speech sound difficulties but the nature of their difficulties will vary as will the impact that their difficulty has on their ability to play, learn, and interact.

Some speech, language, and communication needs will resolve in childhood and others will be lifelong.

The types of speech, language, and communication needs that we may see in the early years are:

- ❖ Difficulties understanding language – understanding what other people say.
- ❖ Difficulties using language – communicating with words and sentences.
- ❖ Difficulty producing speech sounds accurately.
- ❖ Stammering.
- ❖ Voice problems – having a hoarse/croaky voice.
- ❖ Difficulty interacting with others and understanding the social 'rules' of communication.

Early identification is important so that the child can receive appropriate support in a timely fashion and if you have any questions/concerns contact your local speech and language therapy department.

How Might We Observe This in the Early Years?

We have identified what to look out for and why in previous chapters, but it is always important to look at a child holistically. Are they a member of your early years community? Are they accessing their play and learning environment? Do you feel that you need support to understand how the child is learning and developing?

Always raise your concern with other members of your team or, if you work alone, with your support network (keeping the child anonymous). It is likely that other members of the team will have made similar observations and by sharing your thoughts, you can work together to support the child.

How Can We Support the Child with Speech, Language, and Communication Needs in the Setting? Targets and Interventions

Here we have made some suggestions for targets and interventions. These are just examples; it is important that when planning and writing targets for a child's individualised plan that they are specific to that child and we know that each child is unique and the plan must reflect this. We have deliberately written interventions which can be carried out through natural play – it is important that children are not made to feel 'different' by being taken away from their play in which they may be deeply engaged.

Attention and Listening – Why Does This Matter?

Being able to listen to and attend to what other people are saying, and to be able to focus your own attention on play activity, is essential for language learning. Children who are struggling to focus their attention and listening skills are missing out on many opportunities to hear other people talking about their environment and they may miss opportunities to interact and develop relationships with others.

Need of the child	Outcome/target – what do we want the child to achieve?	Actions – advice on achieving the outcomes (Please include ideas that the child and family can do to help achieve these outcomes as well as for those working with the child)
		Attention and Listening
'Child' needs to focus their attention and listening skills so that they can access their learning environment. *What does the child actually need? For example, if child is becoming frustrated because they can't communicate, the need is to communicate their wants and preferences.*	'Child' to focus on an activity of his choice for (number) minutes with/without adult support (enter frequency) by (time scale).	Observe the child and their interests. They are more likely to engage if we are following their lead. Provide toys/resources/opportunities which will engage and interest them. Adult support is not encouraging the child to 'stay for one more minute' but finding opportunities to extend the child's play experience so that they remain engaged for longer.
'Child' needs to...	'Child' to engage in small group activity with/ without adult support by (timescale).	Reflect on what was discussed in Chapter 6 on small group time. This doesn't mean 'adult led' but adults can have an important role in being a part of this group and extending play, communication, and interaction. Find the 'natural' small group time (snack time for example) and support the child to feel part of the group.

Play and Interaction – Why Does This Matter?

We have probably all heard that 'play is children's work' – it is how they learn and then express themselves through their choices and preferences. Play provides opportunities for children to attach meaning to words and to develop other important cognitive skills such as problem solving, memory, and mathematical concepts. Play also provides the opportunity to develop social interaction skills, such as joint attention, sharing, and turn-taking, and to acquire an understanding of empathy and the needs of others.

Speech, Language, and Communication Needs

Play and interaction are the foundation skills upon which language can be built.

Need of the child	Outcome/target – what do we want the child to achieve?	Actions – advice on achieving the outcomes (Please include ideas that the child and family can do to help achieve these outcomes as well as for those working with the child)
		Play and Interaction
'Child' needs to develop relationships with others.	Child will indicate they want another turn using a gesture/sign/word in a repetitive, motivating play activity with an adult by (timescale).	Know the child and what motivates them. Can you find a way to play where you can pause and wait for the child to indicate they want another turn? Tickle games can be a good option, or singing a favourite song – engage the child and then pause the activity. Can they indicate that they want 'more'? Accept non-verbal communication – this could be a body movement or eye contact and model the word you want to hear in that situation – for example, 'more,' 'again.' We want the child to learn that they can have control over their environment and that communication is a useful skill for them to develop and use.
'Child' needs to...	Child will take turns with a peer during a play activity with/without adult support by (timescale).	Natural play is likely to be more engaging for the child, rather than a planned 'turn-taking game.' Know the child – what are they interested in? Can you find opportunities to support turn-taking when the child is playing alongside a peer in a self-chosen play activity? Model turn-taking language – 'James's turn'

Understanding the Environment – Why Does This Matter?

We have already identified that children must feel safe and secure in order to access their learning environment. If a child does not understand the routine of the setting, they may feel angry or anxious and this will be a barrier to their learning as their brain will be in a state of 'fight or flight.'

Take a moment to consider how we feel when we enter a new, unfamiliar situation.

Need of the child	Outcome/target – what do we want the child to achieve?	Actions – advice on achieving the outcomes (Please include ideas that the child and family can do to help achieve these outcomes as well as for those working with the child)
		Understanding the Environment
'Child' needs to understand what is happening in their daily routine.	'Child' to demonstrate an understanding of the daily routine by allowing an adult to lead them to an activity when shown an object of reference/photograph/symbol by (timescale).	It can be helpful to keep objects of reference in a box together where all adults know where to find them. When it is time to transition, take the object to the child; if possible, let them explore the object and take it with them as they transition with you. At this stage you will still gently lead the child by the hand, taking the object of reference with you. Examples of objects of reference may be a plate for snack time, a nappy for when the child needs changing, soap for handwashing, a wellie for going outside. We always add language as we show the child the object – 'snack time' as we show the child the plate. If a child is struggling to follow the routine of the setting, objects of reference will be easier to understand before moving onto photographs and then symbols.
'Child' needs to…	'Child' to demonstrate an understanding of the daily routine by transitioning to an activity when shown an object of reference/photograph/symbol by (timescale).	As above but we are now working towards the child transitioning without being physically led by the adult.

Understanding Language – Why Does This Matter?

Children need to understand what is being said to them so that they can develop their vocabulary and interaction skills. When children struggle to understand what is being said to them, they will struggle to engage with others and will find it difficult to access a learning curriculum and make progress.

Speech, Language, and Communication Needs

Need of the child	Outcome/target – what do we want the child to achieve?	Actions – advice on achieving the outcomes (Please include ideas that the child and family can do to help achieve these outcomes as well as for those working with the child)
		Understanding Language
'Child' needs to understand what is being said to them.	Child will understand instructions containing two keywords by (timescale).	This can be tricky to do 'naturally' but with practice you will find it easier. With these ideas you need to have a choice of at least two items for each underlined word when you give the instruction. You can talk about what you see so that the child hears the language and connects it to what they are looking at/playing with. You can then give the child an instruction. Home corner – 'the <u>apple</u> is on the <u>plate</u>,' 'the <u>pear</u> is in the <u>bowl</u>.' Can you put the <u>pear</u> on the <u>plate</u>?' Small world – 'put the <u>baby</u> on the <u>table</u>,' 'put the <u>mummy</u> on the <u>bed</u>' Outside environment – 'the <u>stick</u> is in the <u>mud</u>,' 'the <u>leaf</u> is in the <u>sand</u>.' 'Can you put the <u>leaf</u> in the <u>mud</u>?' Remember to use play resources that are motivating and interesting to the child.
'Child' needs to understand what is said to them.	Child will understand instructions containing three keywords by (timescale).	As above but there is more to understand here. Home corner – you could fill a bowl with water and some bubble bath. '<u>Wash</u> <u>teddy's</u> <u>nose</u>,' '<u>dry</u> <u>baby's</u> <u>feet</u>.' Outside environment – '<u>kick</u> the <u>ball</u> to <u>Theo</u>,' '<u>throw</u> the <u>beanbag</u> to <u>Daisy</u>.' Remember – you need to ensure there is a choice for each underlined word.

Using Language – Why Does This Matter?

All children need a way to communicate their needs, wants, and preferences. Some children will communicate with sign language or gestures, others may express themselves through pictures and most will learn to communicate using words.

Children who are unable to communicate effectively with others may feel frustrated, isolated, or angry as they struggle to express themselves and get their needs met, and often we will see children communicate these feelings through their behaviour.

Introducing Signing

If children are struggling to express themselves using words, then introducing some simple signs can be really helpful. We only sign key words and we always speak and sign. It is important that we discuss this with parents and offer reassurance that signing does not replace talking. Children will typically use sign until they no longer need to and can use spoken words reliably.

How to Choose Which Signs to Introduce?

This is a discussion to be had with parents/carers. We know that children need to be motivated to communicate, so explore which signs would be useful to the child. What is the child motivated by? What are their main needs and preferences? Who are the important people in their life?

If you have not been trained to use signing, you can research how to sign specific vocabulary and there are demonstrations available on the internet but it would also be a good opportunity to raise the training need with management and a whole team approach to signing is important as we don't want the child to be able to communicate with only one adult.

If you assess that the child needs other ways to communicate – visuals for example, then it is important to liaise with your local speech therapy department so that you can get some support with this.

Top Tip

Children will recognise real objects first (objects of reference), then photographs of real objects, and then symbols. It is useful to know this if we are using visuals to support language understanding and use in our environment.

Need of the child	Outcome/target – what do we want the child to achieve?	Actions – advice on achieving the outcomes
		(Please include ideas that the child and family can do to help achieve these outcomes as well as for those working with the child)
		Using Language
'Child' needs to express their wants, needs and preferences.	Child will indicate a preference using eye pointing/gesture/sign/word when presented with a choice of two items by (timescale).	Making choices helps the child to learn that they can influence what happens around them.
		You can offer a choice between two toys, drinks, or food at snack time and remember to be specific and model the vocabulary we are wanting the child to learn – 'milk or water?' would you like the 'paint or sand?'
		Show the child the item you are offering as you say the word so that the child knows that the word matches the object.
		Accept any non-verbal communication initially as it is important that the child knows that all communication is valued. Always reinforce the vocabulary once a choice has been made, for example, if the child reaches for the milk, you model the word 'milk.'
		Notice – is the child always selecting the item presented second? If so, try using a high motivator and a low motivator (something you know the child likes and something they don't) and swap the order you present the items. If the child communicates that they want the item you know they don't like, still give the selected item and allow time for the child to explore this. Look for the cues that the child does not want this item (noise, rejection of item) and then offer the choice again.

Speech, Language, and Communication Needs

Need of the child	Outcome/target	Actions
'Child' needs to express their wants, needs and preferences.	Child will consistently put two words together in a range of contexts with a range of people by (timescale).	Comment on what the child is doing/playing with using simple language and ideally using two-word phrases. Model two-word phrases in a range of natural situations: snack time – 'more banana,' 'milk gone.' Tidy up time – 'in box,' 'paint gone.' Extend the child's single-word utterances naturally (don't ask them to repeat you). For example, the child says 'baby' you can comment 'baby eating.' Offer choices – if the child is requesting 'more' at the snack table, offer a choice – 'more milk or more water?'

Speech Sounds – Why Does This Matter?

As we have just described, when children are not understood they can become frustrated or withdrawn. Speech sound difficulties can result in a child being unintelligible in severe cases. It is so important that children know that we value what they are saying more than how clear they are saying it. Developing accurate speech sounds is important for future literacy skills. Children need to be able to say sounds accurately so that they can make the sound-letter correspondence when they begin reading and writing. If a child says 'tat' instead of 'cat,' when they come to sound out the letters in order to read and spell they may well 'sound out' 't-a-t,' which does not spell 'cat.'

If children are not understood on a regular basis, their self-esteem and confidence in communicating may be impacted and again may affect their ability to develop relationships with others.

Need of the child	Outcome/target – what do we want the child to achieve?	Actions – advice on achieving the outcomes
'Child' needs to be understood by others.		(Please include ideas that the child and family can do to help achieve these outcomes as well as for those working with the child) **Speech Sounds** We do not often set specific targets for speech sound difficulties in the early years – this is because children need to have well-developed language skills in order to work on specific speech sounds. If you are supporting a child with severe speech sound difficulties, liaise with the child's speech and language therapist about how you can help in the setting. There are many speech sound awareness activities that you can use which will help the child's awareness of sounds – see Chapters 5 and 6 for examples.

Be sure to keep a record of interventions and monitor progress. This is your evidence about the child's development and what support they have received.

It is important to observe the child holistically and we have included a suggested monitoring template:

Child's initial	What was the play session about? (target)	How engaged was the child? 1–5 (1 low, 5 high)	What environment was this in? Inside Outside Set up Natural play Child-led Adult-led Child interest Adult interest	What will the educator/ adult do next time?	Date of this session Time of this session	Date for next sessions	Any comments

Stammering

As we know, language development in the early years can be a complex process for some, whilst for others it can progress very rapidly. As children are developing and refining their speech and language skills, they may hesitate, repeat words or sounds, or they may even repeat whole sentences. This lack of fluency is fairly typical and often children will become more fluent as they settle into their new language skills.

Stammering is the term used for when this pattern of difficulty in getting words out persists and is impacting the child's ability to express themselves.

So when should we be concerned?

As every child is unique and will have their own language profile, if you have observed some non-fluency and you are concerned, please seek advice from your local speech therapy department.

What is our role?

There are things you can do to help...

- ❖ Show the child that you are interested in what they are telling you and not how they are saying it.
- ❖ Be patient and show the child that you are listening.
- ❖ Slow your own rate of speech to provide a calm, less rushed communication environment.
- ❖ Do not finish the child's sentences when they are struggling. You are wanting to help but this can be very frustrating for the child.
- ❖ Do not tell the child to stop and take a breath, this does not help and will interrupt the child's thoughts.

❖ Provide opportunities for the child to contribute and join in without having to talk if they would prefer not to.
❖ Be sure to praise the child for their achievements – 'you were really kind to Jamie by giving him a turn with that toy.'

Selective Mutism

Please remember it is important that we do not diagnose children but we do need to know if the child is just a quiet child or whether there is something else happening.

It is perfectly acceptable to be a quiet child or to be shy in larger groups or with unfamiliar people. We don't need a world of extroverts! But we do need to ensure that children are accessing their learning environment and have a good friend or two. Is the child able to transition from home to the setting without any distress or anxiety? If the answer is yes, and the child is learning and developing and has formed a friendship then we do not need to intervene.

So when should we be concerned?

❖ The child is able to talk freely with certain people but then cannot talk to others.
❖ The child 'freezes' or displays high levels of anxiety when in a situation where there is an expectation to speak.
❖ If the child has been in the setting consistently for longer than a month and is not yet talking in the setting (no concerns regarding language development) but will talk in a different environment (home).

What is our role?

It is important that we do not put pressure on children to talk. Get to know the child by observing their play and interests. Join them and follow their lead, commenting rather than questioning. Respect their choice to move away from you if that is what they do.

The most important thing to note – do not talk about the child not talking in front of them. This is the golden rule for any child but it is so important for children displaying these difficulties. Keep your interactions gentle and natural and seek advice if you are concerned.

Voice

You may notice that the child has a croaky or hoarse voice. You may observe that the child sounds like they are talking through their nose. A croaky or hoarse voice can indicate some vocal cord damage. In young children this is typically a result of persistent shouting or screaming. It is important that parents are supported to seek advice about this as we need to encourage good vocal habits. You can support by using a calm quiet voice (not a whisper as this puts the vocal cords under tension). You can talk about the concept of loud and quiet and encourage all children to use gentle, quiet voices. Access to water to keep the vocal tract hydrated is also important.

If a child sounds like they are talking through their nose or if they sound 'nasal' it may require further investigation – support parents to talk to their health visitor or doctor about this.

Working with Parents and Other Professionals

It can feel daunting speaking to parents about your concerns. You may be the first person to raise a concern about speech, language, and communication and so be mindful of how you introduce this to parents. It is possible that some parents will be upset, some parents may disagree and challenge your observations, and some parents may be relieved that somebody else has seen something that they have been concerned about. You cannot predict how parents will react.

With this in mind, these top tips may help:

- State the facts – there is no need to hypothesise or diagnose. Just describe to the parents what you have observed and how this is impacting the child.
- Ensure parents have ample opportunity to raise concerns to the team.
- Always ask for consent if making a referral – be clear as to why you are making the referral and what you hope to achieve by making the referral.
- Children often present differently at home and in nursery. Parents may be surprised at your observation and it is really important that we listen to how the child presents at home and welcome parents sharing examples and information with us.
- Be honest.

Working with other professionals is important when supporting children with speech, language, and communication needs. There are a variety of professionals who may become involved – speech and language therapists, educational psychologists, health visitors, and advisory teachers are the most likely to be involved. Remember that you are an **equal member** of the team supporting the child together with the parents, with every member of the child's 'team' bringing different information and skills, and it is vital that all members of the 'team' are given the opportunity to share their information and recommendations, always keeping the child at the centre of any decisions/plans.

INDEX

babbling 8, 31, 34, 38, 47, 94

cause and effect 7, 36, 45
commenting 9–10, 38, 50, 140
conversations 10–11, 116
copying 33, 37–8, 46

describing 32–3, 38, 103–4
dummies 94–5, 125

eating 39–45, 101, 124
eye contact 7, 43, 45–6, 58, 72, 105, 119
eye pointing 4, 31, 35, 96

facial expressions 7–8, 11, 14, 89, 119
families 67–8, 81–3, 90–3, 107, 114–15
free-flow 49
friendships 10, 87, 118
fronting 78, 105

gestures 31, 34, 72–3, 96

hearing 6, 14, 45

interactions 118; adult-child 37–9, 46, 65, 79, 89–90, 140; quality 31–2, 43, 58; social 14–15

keywords 8, 10, 70

listening 6–7, 36–7, 59–60, 132

messy play 33
modelling 8, 37, 78, 98, 106
motivation 97
music 33, 39, 59–60

names 68
nappy changing 32, 62, 83

painting 39, 86
parents 46, 91–2, 141
peer observations 20–4
positioning 46, 89–90

reading 116, 126–7
repetition 8–9, 36, 60, 70, 118
role play 33–6, 106

selective mutism 140
signing 136–7
sleep 32, 37
speech and language therapists 15–16, 94, 141
stammering 139–40
stopping 78, 105

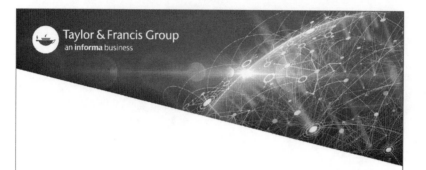